W9-AQM-802

THE CARLYLES

A biography of Thomas and Jane Carlyle

By the same author

SHAW
FORWARD TO NATURE
FAREWELL TO ARGUMENT
THE SOUNDING CATARACT
AN IRISHMAN'S ENGLAND
AN ARTIST OF LIFE
MARRIAGE AND GENIUS
LEO TOLSTOY

BOUND UPON A COURSE
WHILE FOLLOWING THE PLOUGH
DOWN TO EARTH
THE TRIUMPH OF THE TREE
THE MOVING WATERS
PATHS OF LIGHT

A portrait of Carlyle by Whistler

[*Glasgow Art Gallery and Museum*]

THE CARLYLES

A biography of
Thomas and Jane Carlyle

John Stewart Collis

Dodd, Mead & Company
New York

© John Stewart Collis 1971
All rights reserved
No part of this book may be reproduced in any form
without permission in writing from the publisher
First published in the United States of America 1973
ISBN 0.396.06637.2
Library of Congress Catalog Card Number 72–2555

Printed in Great Britain

PR
4433
.C57

Contents

Illustrations

Preface

In studying the admirable biographies of Thomas Carlyle and Jane Welsh Carlyle, I have missed a truly succinct, yet comprehensive, account of their joint upbringing, courtship, and subsequent life together. It has seemed to me that if the material were sufficiently mastered and digested, it should be possible to unfold a swiftly-moving tight narration from first to last with its ever-increasing drama, at the same time including Carlyle's *oeuvre* and what he aimed to say as chief message but didn't, and, what I have not seen discerned with appropriate emphasis, his desperate hour of decision. This is what is attempted here.

JOHN STEWART COLLIS

'... one of the most complex, one of the most perplexing, one of the most fascinating and tragic personalities of world literature.'
Professor Charles Sarolea in 1931

'My dear, whatever you do, never marry a man of genius.'
Jane Carlyle to John Sterling

1   *The Father*

'HE was among the last of the true men, which Scotland (on the old system) produced, or can produce.' Thus wrote Thomas Carlyle (1795–1881) of his father, James Carlyle, a builder at Ecclefechan. And again, 'Alas: such is the *mis*-education of these days, it is only among what are called the *un*-educated classes (those educated by experience that you can look for a *man*. My father, in several respects, has not, that I can think of, left his fellow.'

This birth into a family of Lowland Scottish peasant stock is very important, for such families were often aristocratic in their demeanour and their values. Carlyle talks of his father as the last of such men. But that is a pardonable exaggeration. The type still exists, however fast it may be disappearing; while in the nineteenth century there were not a few naturally cultivated families remarkable for their dignity, independence of spirit, high principles by which conduct should be guided, and often a powerful felicity in verbal expression. James Carlyle was a very strong personality, and he set certain standards which became embedded deeply in his son. One of these was the Gospel of Work: the great thing to do in life is to work well and truly. This is one ideal and a fine one, but it can never be an absolute. If most of us were to enter the Leisure State it would be awkward as such. Carlyle took it over as an absolute, and made his name immortal, but his life unhappy.

According to Carlyle, his father possessed wonderful powers of expression, though not on paper. 'He was a man of *the* very largest natural endowment of any it has been my lot to converse with: none of us will ever forget that bold glowing style of his, flowing free from the untutored Soul; full of metaphors (though he knew not what a metaphor was) with all manner of potent words ... Nothing did I ever hear him undertake to render visible, which did not become almost ocularly so. Never shall we again hear such speech as that was: the whole district knew of it.' Interesting words: the son seems to have been the father, as it were, made free by education. To render things visible is the chief mark of Carlyle's literary genius. The fault of the father was that he exaggerated 'yet only in description and for the sake chiefly of *humorous* effect' – which again exactly describes the son's best literary efforts. However, James Carlyle, though open to general ideas, shut his mind against poetry and fiction, treating both as false and criminal. He was deeply shocked at old Thomas Carlyle for reading the *Arabian Nights*. He refused to be interested in Burns who just then was at the height of his fame. The Labour politician, David Kirkwood, in his autobiography, gives a sample of *his* father's manner of speaking: he said to his son on the subject of Burns and David, 'Men of the soil they were, my cullan, and of the open field; where secrets are as fully revealed by a drab o' dew on a blade of grass as by the limitless constellations of the heavens. They were baith sinners as they were baith sinners by the same sinning. They were baith members of a race that was faur doon the brae, and by each of them was the nation set high amang the nations of the world. One cam' to be the national king of the Jews and the ither the national hero of the Scots. If ye learn the psalms of David and the poems of Robert Burns, ye'll have a thockt ready for every incident, grave or gay, that may come to ye in life.' James Carlyle, though perhaps equally eloquent on themes such as Wisdom and Truth and Conduct, could never have held such a view. He was afraid where it might lead him. 'As a man of Speculation,' says his son, '(had Culture ever unfolded him) he must have gone wild and desperate as Burns: but he was a man of Conduct, and Work keeps all right.'

But he was determined that his son Thomas should be

unfolded by Culture, and be educated out of his small funds, thereby causing undying gratitude in that son. Both mother and father wanted him to become a minister of the Church; but when he boggled at this when it came to the point, and then boggled at school-mastering, and for a long period appeared to be doing nothing of worth, James Carlyle never uttered a single word of reproach, never offended his son's *amour propre*, but waited patiently for him to find himself. Perhaps this gives us the best insight into the father's character.

His other traits were less uncommon among men of his period and circumstance. He was choleric and irascible without benefit of drink. His authority in the household was absolute, and the family dreaded his wrath : 'their wish was not in the matter. It was not a joyful life.' He was intemperate in general abstemiousness. He did not encourage chatter, and his children feared his 'tongue-paralyzing cold indifferent "Hah".' No one dared love him freely. He could not unbosom himself, he could not freely show affection, it was as if his heart were walled in. His wife suffered from this. He only showed his feelings once, in a paroxysm of grief, throwing himself on the floor, when she was ill – a scene she did not witness. Again, this trait informed the famous son, and caused much suffering.

This was the element in which Carlyle was brought up – a household in which Religion and Conduct and Work were the absolutes. An atmosphere of thrift and habitual frugality. A diet of porridge and potatoes – for months on end, even when unnecessary. No political revolutionary views were held by the father, but he knew that great changes in society must come. In the years between 1799–1800, when oatmeal was as high as ten shillings a stone, he had noticed labourers retire, each separately to a brook, and there *drink* instead of dine; and he had declared that 'the lot of the poor man was growing worse and worse; that the world could not and would not last as it was; but mighty changes, of which none saw the end, were on the way'.

James Carlyle did not remain a builder. He became a master-mason, though the largest sum he earned in one year was £100 – for building Cressfield House. But when show and cheapness began to be preferred to *substance* in the mason trade he quitted it and became a farmer at Mainhill. In this he 'struggled with his old valour, and here too prevailed'. And with the bare funds possible he determined that Thomas should be educated.

He remained an inspiring example to Carlyle of how to live. 'Let me write my Books as he built his Houses,' he said.

cheapness began to be preferred to *substance* in the mason trade he quitted it and became a farmer at Mainhill. In this he 'struggled with his old valour, and here too prevailed'. And with the bare funds possible he determined that Thomas should be educated.

He remained an inspiring example to Carlyle of how to live. 'Let me write my Books as he built his Houses,' he said.

unfolded by Culture, and be educated out of his small funds, thereby causing undying gratitude in that son. Both mother and father wanted him to become a minister of the Church; but when he boggled at this when it came to the point, and then boggled at school-mastering, and for a long period appeared to be doing nothing of worth, James Carlyle never uttered a single word of reproach, never offended his son's *amour propre*, but waited patiently for him to find himself. Perhaps this gives us the best insight into the father's character.

His other traits were less uncommon among men of his period and circumstance. He was choleric and irascible without benefit of drink. His authority in the household was absolute, and the family dreaded his wrath : 'their wish was not in the matter. It was not a joyful life.' He was intemperate in general abstemiousness. He did not encourage chatter, and his children feared his 'tongue-paralyzing cold indifferent "Hah".' No one dared love him freely. He could not unbosom himself, he could not freely show affection, it was as if his heart were walled in. His wife suffered from this. He only showed his feelings once, in a paroxysm of grief, throwing himself on the floor, when she was ill – a scene she did not witness. Again, this trait informed the famous son, and caused much suffering.

This was the element in which Carlyle was brought up – a household in which Religion and Conduct and Work were the absolutes. An atmosphere of thrift and habitual frugality. A diet of porridge and potatoes – for months on end, even when ... essary. No political revolutionary views were held by the father, but he knew that great changes in society must come. In the years between 1799–1800, when oatmeal was as high as ten shillings a stone, he had noticed labourers retire, each separately to a brook, and there *drink* instead of dine; and he had declared that 'the lot of the poor man was growing worse and worse; that the world could not and would not last as it was; but mighty changes, of which none saw the end, were on the way'.

James Carlyle did not remain a builder. He became a master-mason, though the largest sum he earned in one year was £100 – for building Cressfield House. But when show and may attain to literary fame; and though starvation be my lot, I will smile that I have not been born a king.'

During the vacations he joined his parents at Mainhill, for it was at this period that his father had turned farmer. The house, set in a bleak and windy spot, had to hold six others, three sons and three daughters, so it is not surprising that the only secluded spot he could find in which to study was a ditch, and that it was in this ditch (a dry one) that he read *Faust* in the original. The parents somehow managed to clothe and feed the lot, the food chiefly consisting of oatmeal, milk, and potatoes. The brothers and sisters were all hard at work, the little ones at school, the elders in the field or dairy, and in the intervals reading history, or Scott's novels, or attempting geometry. We get a glimpse of the Carlylean atmosphere through a letter to Carlyle from his sister Mary, then twelve years old. 'The boys and I are employed this winter in waiting on the cattle, and are going on very well at present. I generally write a copy every night, and read a little in the *Cottagers of Glenburnie*, or some such like; and it shall be my earnest desire never to imitate the abominable slutteries of Mrs Maclarty... In the meantime I shall endeavour to be a good girl, to be kind and obedient to my parents, and obliging to my brothers and sisters.'

If when reading these words, we, in our time and place, hold it against Mary that she wrote like that, and are inclined to wish that she had imitated the abominable slutteries of Mrs Maclarty (whoever she may have been), we should remember that the way of writing belonged to the period. Here is Carlyle himself writing to his mother at about this time. 'There are few things in this world more valuable than knowledge, and youth is the period for acquiring it. With the exception of the religious and moral instruction which I had the happiness of receiving from my parents, and which I humbly trust will not be entirely lost on me, there is nothing for which I feel more grateful than for the education which they have bestowed upon me.'

The mothers of remarkable men are almost always themselves remarkable. Carlyle's mother was no exception. Her strength of character was very evident. She had not been taught to write, but learned to do so in order to be able to communicate with Thomas (the eldest, there were three other sons, and three daughters); and her letters, which have been preserved, are touching in their anxiety for his spiritual welfare. 'Seek God with all your heart; and oh, my dear son, cease not to pray for His counsel in all your ways... I beg you not to neglect reading part of your Bible daily.' He always took it well and promised to do as she said. In his early youth, he sometimes alarmed her with a question such as 'Did Jesus really make wheelbarrows?', but he soon learned to be more tactful. He was devoted to her to the end – his deep attachment unmarred by complex. Her piety was not accompanied with sanctimoniousness, nor her goodness with hypocrisy, nor her virtue with virtuousness. She could be forthright enough : 'Weel, Agg, lass, I've never spoken to ye sin ye stole our coals,' she said to a certain Agg Byers. 'I'll gie ye an advice; never steal nae more.' But she worked too hard : the burden of keeping things going was too great. At one time she had a mental breakdown, and they feared for her sanity, but she recovered and again became the household pillar.

One of the things which caused her strain was Carlyle's uncertainty of aim and disinclination to 'go into the Ministry'. That he should train for the Church and become an eminent Divine was her great hope; in fact, it was the general aim at that time of poor Scottish parents who had a son worth educating. In this he disappointed her. He began to find that, though a born preacher, he had not the least desire for the Ministry. The era of dogma-doubt had just then begun to set in with severity, and Carlyle was a typical example of the intellectual no longer able to respond to beliefs which had been taken without discomfort or question for so long. Soon after leaving the University, he was obliged to tell his parents definitely that he could not pursue theology. His father curbed his disappointment and his tongue, uttering not one word to dissuade him from the decision : his mother had plenty to say and made it hard for him. He took up schoolmastering, but he hated it. He could not bear spending precious hours teaching Latin and Arithmetic to stupid boys when he was burning to devour books for his own ends. He gave

✪

2   *The Son*

JAMES CARLYLE made his decision about his son's education with
resolution, for Thomas's superiority, his unusualness, was sensed
by all. Luckily, he was also clever in the school manner: he
might have been stupid academically, bad at examinations, a
'small-Latin-and-less-Greek' man in spite of good schooling. As
it happened, the family never regretted the decision; for he was a
natural scholar eagerly devouring anything put before him by
school teachers who regarded him as a hopeless case of
precocity, and were perturbed by his questions. He had learned
to read so early that he could not recall the year. When
Thomas was five, his father taught him arithmetic at which he
showed extraordinary capacity, and he was too advanced in
Latin for the masters at his first school (Ecclefechan). So he went
to a Grammar School at Annan. There he had a bad time with
the other boys, for that 'something unusual about him' offended
them and they bullied him. His mother had made him promise
never to hit back, but hold faithfully to the Christian principle of
turning the other cheek. Happily, nature asserted itself, and one
day he fought back successfully, after which he was not molested
again (so we are told; though there is always something of the
mythical in such claims).

He went to the University at Edinburgh at the age of
fourteen, for in those days students were more advanced and
adult, as well as far more serious and self-disciplined – and it was
the Scotland of the nineteenth century when education was a
passion. Edinburgh was a hundred miles from Ecclefechan.
Carlyle did not travel there by train or bus or coach – he
walked. He walked twenty miles a day for five days, and the
same back at the vacation.

Such earnestness and discipline merited good teaching, but

5

Carlyle later declared that it was his painful duty to asser
'ours was the worst of all hitherto discovered universities'. N
theless, he was at 'a seat of learning', and could sit down
learn, even if he did most of the teaching himself. 'Home.
learnt to read in the original with difficulty,' he says, 'Aeschylu
and Sophocles mainly in translations. Tacitus and Virgil became
really interesting to me.' He thought Horace too egoistical and
Cicero too windy. In arithmetic he felt that he made swift
progress, for he loved the subject because of its 'certainties'.
Geometry, for the same reason, also shone before him and
beckoned him on; but after a few years other things of more
pregnant inquiry began to engross him. The great fact was that
the University Library was at his disposal. Thus he could lay
down the foundation for a literary life. 'I learned on my own
strength to read fluently in almost all cultivated languages, on
almost all subjects and sciences.'

His companions, if not equally gifted, were as earnest and full
of high endeavour as he. Some of them took their cue from him,
sensing in him, as so many did, a superior mind. It is well to
mark this, for throughout his life he was always thus regarded by
people drawn from every rank; but these boys had nothing to go
on in the way of works or reputation, only the young Carlyle
himself, and they foretold future greatness and fame for him
while he was still a mere boy. When on vacation they exchanged
letters. There is nothing priggish or too high-toned about these
letters, they are delightful and show how much Carlyle was *liked*
as a humorous as well as an earnest person. 'Your letters will
always be a feast to me,' wrote one friend, 'a happy flow of
language either for pathos, description, or humour, and an easy,
graceful current of ideas appropriate to every subject, character-
ize your style.' He preserved such letters. His own were lost, but
one remains, and it includes these words – 'Oh, Fortune! thou
that givest unto each his portion in this dirty planet, bestow (if it
shall please thee) coronets and crowns, and principalities, and
purses, and pudding, and powers upon the great and noble and
fat ones of the earth. Grant me that, with a heart of independence unyielding to thy favours and unbending to thy frowns, I

it up. Once again, his father did not reproach him, faithfully
believing that his son would work things out in time. How about
the law? Could he not become a great advocate? Many thought
so. And had not the present Chief Advocate raised himself 'from
being a disconsolate preacher'? And seeing that legal affairs left
much room for moral improvement, he could *reform* the Law?
But soon law also was out. By 1820 he was disgusted with it.

This was not waywardness, nor lack of aim. It is the old story
of genius during the uncertain hours. A genius differs from
others in this – that besides the ordinary difficulties of life, he has
to grapple with a force within himself which refuses to be
denied. He feels that he has it in him to conquer the world, and
possibly some lunar ones as well. There is no time to waste.
Almost any job seems terribly in the way, a fearful frustration,
for he is in a tearing hurry. He is in a perpetual state of nervous
tension. Can he do it? He has no confidence in success. He has
boundless humility and yet boundless pride. Ever before him
looms the possibility that things will *not* go right, and that he
will be foiled. Writing about Dickens in his youth, the 'furious
sense of frustration; a spirit like a wild beast in a cage', G. K.
Chesterton said, 'It was only a small matter in the external and
obvious sense; it was only Dickens prevented from being
Dickens.' Carlyle had nothing like so bad a time as Dickens in
his youth; but his fear of losing his way and his time in the
endeavour to find himself was just as great – there was always the
fearful possibility that Carlyle would be prevented from being
Carlyle.

3 *The Friend*

CARLYLE admits that at this period he was a fairly unpleasant sort of person, shy and grossly self-assertive at the same time, intensely vulnerable and also bitterly sarcastic, sometimes regarding himself as an insignificant worm – or thinking that others so regarded him – and then suddenly turning that worm into a torpedo. A clear image is revealed by a letter to him at this time (and evidently kept for posterity) from Margaret Gordon. Carlyle was never blind to feminine beauty or indifferent to an attractive woman who showed interest in him. Miss Gordon was a high-born lady whose young men must have 'prospects', according to the mode of the period, prospects which ought not to be literary ones. Firm nineteenth-century aunts stood behind such girls to prevent inadvisable engagements, and the young lady would be obliged to say farewell to the unprospective young man, perhaps couching her letter in terms of an affectionate 'sister'. Miss Gordon came out strong under this head. Having rebuked him for the regrettable *weakness* which he had evidently displayed towards her, she finally took leave of him in proper style:

> 'And now, my dear friend, a long, long adieu; one advice, and as a parting one consider, value it. Cultivate the milder dispositions of your heart. Subdue the more extravagant visions of the brain. In time your abilities must be known. Among your acquaintance they are already beheld with wonder and delight. By those whose opinion will be valuable, they hereafter will be appreciated. Genius will render you great. May virtue render you beloved! Remove the awful distance between you and ordinary men by kind and gentle manners. Deal gently with their inferiority, and be convinced they will

respect you as much and like you more. Why conceal the real goodness that lies in your heart? I have ventured this counsel from an anxiety for your future welfare, and I would enforce it with all the earnestness of the most sincere friendship.'

Whatever we may think regarding the manner and the condescension of this letter, we must admire the perspicacity of Miss Gordon as to Carlyle's character and his future. We can be wise after the event. We know what Queen Victoria and Disraeli and Count Bismarck eventually said to Carlyle. She did not. He was only twenty-two years old at the time.

Nor could he know. There was no promise, no brightness in the sky. He made diligent and desperate literary efforts, 'but of such a futile, dismal, lonely, dim, and chaotic kind, in a sense all ghastly chaos to me. Sad, dim, and ugly as the shore of Styx and Phlegethon.' Yet light did shine upon him. Help and encouragement did come to him in the shape of a friend whose memory he was to cherish for ever.

An attractive aspect of Carlyle is that he was always able to make and to retain men friends (in contrast with Strindberg and even Tolstoy). Earliest of these, and to him ever the foremost, was Edward Irving. This man was some five years his senior. He had preceded him at Annan School and thence to Edinburgh University. Irving was the kind of shooting star whom people gaze at with fascination : a man of compelling aspect, well-built and handsome, of splendid personal address : at school and university brilliantly clever and examination-passing : as a schoolmaster formidable : later on earnest and religious without theological doubts, becoming a celebrated preacher with flocks of folk, many high-born and high-placed, audient and subservient to him. He was what we call nowadays a Personality, easily over-shadowing the lasting men, and soon perishing as a person. In fact, the pressure and the popularity proved too much for him, and he went mad and died young. Yet he lives on in the portrait which Carlyle gave of him in the incomparable *Reminiscences*.

It might be thought that such a man as Irving would have

had no time for such a person as Carlyle, so uncouth, so difficult, and such a slow starter. But after an awkward first meeting he sensed the greatness and the genius in the young Carlyle, and did two great things for him : one practical, and the other spiritual. It was through Irving that he became tutor to the sons of the Bullers. Though hating schoolmastering, the possibility of acting as a tutor sometimes came up for consideration. An offer was made to him in 1820 by a Yorkshire farmer to tutor his son for £150 a year. He went and had a look at the youth, and reported his opinion in a letter to a friend. He was glad that he had gone to see, he explained, for 'from description I was ready to accept the place; from inspection all Earnsdale would not have hired me to accept it. This boy was a dotard, a semi-vegetable, the elder brother, head of the family, a two-legged animal without feathers, intellect, or virtue.' They could eat pudding, 'but had no higher power'. However, he was glad to accept the post of tutor at £200 a year to the sons of the Bullers, whom he acknowledged as exceptional. He said that teaching the boys was a pleasure more than a task, and that the eldest was one of the cleverest boys he had ever seen. He was stimulated by the good-breeding of Mr and Mrs Buller, who treated him with respect and esteem. This was a wonderful break. At about the same time he began to get work in the Reviews of the day for translations from the German, and was beginning to be regarded as the British pioneer of German Literature. One might have supposed that this would have encouraged belief in himself – and it is certainly remarkable that an Annandale peasant's son should be thus regarded. But no, he remained without confidence that he would ever attract readers with original work. Irving, however, never wavered in his belief in his friend. He assured him again and again that a glorious future lay before him, he exhorted him not to worry about the unphilosophical, unthinking drivellers who surround and discourage any man of genius, he recognized that his mind had 'taken in so wide a range of study as to be almost incapable of professional trammels'. Indeed Irving was a true friend to him and though Carlyle was not ordinarily a grateful man, and in fact stained his name with records of kindness lavishly bestowed upon him, ungraciously received, and soon ungratefully forgotten, yet in the case of Edward Irving, in spite of everything, he always remained grateful to him, always loving, and treasured his memory to the end of his life.

✺

4 *Jane Baillie Welsh*

CARLYLE never went wife-hunting. Far from it. Nor does it appear that any woman ever went husband-hunting in his direction. But now he came upon a woman whom he felt compelled to marry, however hard he strove not to do so; and who felt compelled to marry him, however frantically she sought to reject him.

Jane Baillie Welsh was born in 1801, thus being six years younger than Carlyle. Her birthplace was the county town of East Lothian, called Haddington, one of the oldest Royal Burghs in Scotland. Her father was a doctor, a dominant figure in the neighbourhood, complete master in his own house, a disciplinarian who was yet adored by both wife and daughter. 'He was of noble and distinguished presence, tall, highly graceful, self-possessed, spontaneously dignified, so that people, if he entered the theatre or the like, asked Who is it?' says Carlyle in the *Reminiscences*. He had 'black hair, bright hazel eyes, bright, lively, steadily expressive features. His medical sagacity was reckoned at a higher and higher rate, medical and other honesty as well; for it was by no means as a wise physician only, but as an honourable, exact, and quietly-dignified man, punctual, faithful in all points, that he was esteemed in the country.' Mrs Welsh was also a striking personality, as excessively feminine as her husband was masculine. She took advantage of her charm and beauty to be wayward, and according to her father-in-law could pass through fifteen different humours in a single evening.

Sometimes children inherit the worst qualities of their parents; but Jane does seem to have combined the best, especially the charm of the mother and the grit of the father. She was an only child and could scarcely avoid being spoilt and regarded as an extraordinary being – which was true. It was the era when the

education of a promising child was started young. James Mill
was taught Greek at the age of three, and punished severely
when he made mistakes. Jane was put to school before the age of
five, and developed such a passion for Euclid that she would
start work at 5 a.m., using as alarm clock a weight tied to her
ankle. Then she acquired a desire to learn Latin, and at the age
of nine was reading Virgil in the original. Indeed her Latin
studies were so far from academic that she became imbued with
the Roman spirit. If she caught herself tempted to do some
cowardly or selfish thing, she would say to herself, 'A Roman
wouldn't have done it'; or, if something heroic, she would think
to herself, 'I have deserved well of the Republic'. It had been far
from easy to persuade her parents to let her learn Latin. At last,
one evening, having hidden herself under a table at which they
were sitting, she had suddenly exclaimed *'Penna – pennae!'* –
and jumping up cried out, 'I want to learn Latin. Please let me
be a boy!' Her father felt obliged to agree to her learning Latin,
though her mother was very much against it, fearing such
knowledge would make her unmarriageable. Such was Jane's
mental grit and determination. Consider this also : what could
be more intimidating to a child than an advancing and truculent
turkey-cock? That angry eye, that beastly beak, that disgraceful
neck, alarms most of us at any age. Such a one, as tall as herself,
got in her path each day she went to school, running at her
gabbling and swelling as if pumped up with air. One day she
reversed this, dashed at it instead, caught it by the neck and
threw it down. A small incident, but indicative of the courage
with which she was to face that long endurance test, her life.

It began so brightly. Her devoted nurse and companion,
Betty, described her as 'a fleein', dancin', lightheartit thing that
naething would have daunted'. The very sight of her, scamper-
ing along to school, her dark eyes bright with mischief and
liveliness, warmed all who saw her. It is important to remember
this morning brightness, for that Haddington nurse, Betty, immediately went on to say : 'But she grew grave a' at once. There
was Maister Irving, ye ken, that had been her teacher; and he
cam' aboot her. Then there was Maister ——. Then there was

Maister Carlyle himsel', and he cam' to finish her off like.'*
She may have appeared to become grave all at once, but it is
unquestionable that, as Froude says, 'her nature at bottom had a
seriousness too deep for words'. Meanwhile she had the world
before her as a brilliant child, that wonderful period when, if
nothing yet is won, nothing is lost, no fearful mistake has been
made, everything is possible, and the tragedy of life is a splendid
romance. Already at the age of thirteen Jane had written a
five-act Tragedy in such high spirits that no characters were left
alive at the end to speak the Epilogue.

By about the age of eighteen one of her relatives dropped the
remark that 'every man who spoke to her for five minutes felt
bound to propose'. She had little beauty in the conventional
sense. Hers was a very small face with a curiously gypsy-like
cast, and her complexion was sallow. Sometimes all that is wrong
with a woman is simply that she lacks charm. After all, that is a
force; to 'utter a charm' is to make some sort of a spell, to use
magic. A lively charming manner is really all that is necessary. It
calls for intelligence and self-assurance, while good breeding
helps a lot. Jane had plenty of this touch of magic at her disposal.
It was easy for men to be deluded by her provoking, sympathetic, excessively thoughtful eyes – and then, observing her
obstinate, too capricious lips, wonder just how they stood with
her. However, it is pleasant to learn that before she began to
realize her power over men, she felt men's power over her in a
pleasantly conventional manner. At the age of nine she adored
soldiers, her first love being an artillery man whose regiment was
temporarily posted in the town. All she wanted was his portrait,
for to come into his presence would be too much. This worship
of soldiers lasted well into her sixteenth year. She would send
proposals of marriage to the officers' quarters, and was not put
off by receiving in return a half-crown or piece of barley sugar.

In 1811, when she was ten, Dr Welsh engaged Edward Irving
to act as classical tutor to her, between school hours. She
admired this handsome, learned, earnest man, and he found in
her a most promising character to shape educationally. Their

* See Robert Nicol's biography in English Men of Letters Series, p. 42

affectionate companionship lasted less than a year. When they met again some years later he fell in love with her – but before that time he had become engaged to a Miss Martin. Jane returned his love passionately, and would gladly have married him, but he was held to his engagement, and he introduced her to Carlyle, without letting him know the strength of their attachment.

When she reached marriageable age she was a difficult woman to pin down. She was not only exceedingly eligible, but also an heiress. Her father died when she was eighteen. This was a severe blow. If a close relation between father and daughter is not rare, the bond was unusually strong in this case. She regarded him with perhaps an excess of veneration and pride. He had wanted a son, but was fully aware that his daughter was exceptional. He felt that this put her in danger. A mistake in her case – especially a mistake in choosing a husband – would be more serious than for a commonplace woman. One day he had asked her to accompany him on a long drive, and had warned her about this, and had spoken of his high hopes and expectations concerning her. This conversation was the closest and most tender she had ever had with him, and eternally memorable to her. Within three days he was dead. He was only forty-three. He had bequeathed the estate of Craigenputtock and most of his money (beyond a small annuity for his wife) to Jane, since he had not anticipated an early death. It is painful to think how much suffering Jane would have been spared if he had lived another twenty or thirty years.

Since she was so eligible now, she became ready to consider suitors, for marriage offered the only escape from the confined activities of Haddington; and though she threw herself into further study, including French and Italian, and read prodigiously, she could not cope with the dullness. She was very attached to her mother but found it hard to deal with her tantrums.

She had no lack of admirers. Few of them found it easy to please her. Her cast of mind was sharp, her angle acute. She permitted no liberties from amorous fools. She was not kind in her observations freely expressed to intimates in correspondence. In her twentieth year she was already in command of a prose style which found its best form in letter writing, and at length became incomparable. This is to her friend Bess Stoddart about a fumbling suitor, in 1821 :

'He came; arrived at the George Inn at eleven o'clock at night, twelve hours after he received my answer to his letter; slept there more soundly, according to his own statement, *"than was to be expected, all the circumstances of the case considered"*, and in the morning sent a few nonsensical lines to announce his nonsensical arrival. Mother and I received him more politely "than was to be expected, all the circumstances of the case considered", and we proceeded to walk, and play at battledore, and talk inanities, about new novels, and new belles, and what had gone on at a splendid party the night before, where he had been (he told us) for half an hour *with his arm under his hat*; and then he corrected himself, and said, *with his head under his arm*! It was of very little consequence where his head was; it is not much worth; but the Lord defend me from visitors so equipped, when I come to give parties. Before dinner he retired to his Inn, and vapoured back, in the course of an hour or so, in all the pride of two waistcoats (one of figured velvet, another of sky-blue satin), gossamer silk stockings, and morocco slippers.'

She must have encouraged him a little, for he returned in a day or two, apparently assuming that she might have changed her mind towards him. 'Ass! I change my mind indeed!'

Such was the strain of mockery in which she spoke of inferior admirers. Her father need not have worried; she was not going to be easy to get. She was far from unduly modest. For a glorious brief period she was on top. Here was no vessel of clay, but a cup of pure gold filled with pure wine. She could take down the moon. She could light a candle off the stars. Why should she marry anything less than the ideal? A Byron might serve, she thought, but where was he to be had? Rousseau's *La Nouvelle*

Heloïse provided her with a standard at this time. She wrote to Bess:

'One serious bad consequence will result to you from reading *Heloïse*, at least if your soul-strings are screwed up to the same key as mine. Alas! I told you I should die a virgin, if I reached *twenty in vain*. Even so will it prove. This Book, this fatal Book, has given me the idea of a love so *pure* (yes, you may laugh! but I repeat it), so pure, so constant, so disinterested, so exalted, that no love the men of this world can offer me will ever fill up the picture my imagination has drawn with the help of Rousseau. No lover will Jane Welsh ever find like St Preux, no husband like Wolmar (I don't mean to insinuate that I *should like both*): and to no man will she ever give her heart and pretty hand who bears to these no resemblance. George Rennie! James Aitken! Robert MacTurk! James Baird! ! ! Robby Angus! – O Lord! Where is the St Preux? Where is the Wolmar? Bess, I am in earnest – I shall never marry.'

5   The Meeting

EDWARD IRVING had an unfortunate manner of expressing himself. After he had lost Jane Welsh as a possible wife, he wrote, 'She contemplates the inferiority of others rather from the point of view of ridicule and contempt than from that of commiseration and relief; and by so doing she not only leaves objects in distress and loses the luxury of doing good, but she contracts in her own mind a degree of coldness and bitterness which suits ill with my conception of female character and a female's position in society.' He did not understand Jane Welsh. She enjoyed ridiculing people, and did so all her life; she was capable of bitterness and vindictiveness, I am glad to say, since this generally goes with characters capable of intense gratitude and affection; but there was nothing cold about her, nothing superficial. Those who enjoy mockery often prize sincerity above all things. She met Carlyle in June 1821. And he had an abundance of sincerity!

It was a conventional first meeting. Irving proudly introduced her to him. He addressed proper remarks to Mrs Welsh, whose appearance made him nervous, and after she had retired they talked a little, and then they left. Carlyle had seen her. She had turned her eyes to him. The rest followed. In that period and in those circles you didn't make a 'date'. There was a way open to cultivated people which served well enough. You sent music or books to the young lady, with a little note.

Carlyle did this after their second meeting, which was more fruitful than the first. He had no small talk, but given a chance his conversation was captivating. We learn this from many sources in the years of his fame, and it seems that, even at this early age, his tongue was compelling. So was his personality. He had the poet's eye, as romantically conceived, with fire and movement in the depths as his spirit stirred. He was tall and ungainly, in the attractive Abraham Lincoln manner. His brown hair was disarranged over a high, climbing forehead. He had a broad Annandale accent – but this did not count in his favour among the Scottish gentry. This second evening he put up a good performance in fine talk. Jane was no mean conversationalist herself, and was to become wonderful at narrating the small exchanges of life – which chiefly make the sum of life. But she let him hold the stage, and listened raptly, ready to read deep meaning into dark sayings and runic prophecies of woe. She was amazed by the wide range of his mind and the singular angle of his approach. She wanted, indeed she yearned, to have a man of genius for a husband. That was her simplicity. She was a mocking-bird. She could be highly sarcastic at the expense of other people. But she was romantic. She was unable to envisage the actual. Deeply sincere, *au fond,* and with a passion for the life of the mind, she longed for a literary genius as her partner. It would be so exciting and worthwhile. There would be such wonderful conversations, and such stirring evenings with celebrities come to hold converse with her famous husband; occasions when she would be in her element as hostess, and would shine as brightly as he. She imagined the children also, who would obviously be remarkable offspring.

At first she did not feel that Carlyle altogether fulfilled this ideal. It was not that she questioned, as she should have done, the advent of children or the swiftness of his attainment to fame, position, and money. But her literary genius should also be elegant and have an upper-class accent. In this respect Carlyle was lacking. In addition to his accent he was uncouth. He didn't seem to know how to manage his arms and legs while in company, and kicked the fire-tongs, and handled tea-cups in a manner which irritated her.

In any case, rejoicing in her position of much sought-after young lady, she had no intention of encouraging Carlyle too much too soon. She had a passion for George Rennie : her letters make it quite plain that she was in love with him even if she did not love him – but the dangerous thrill of the former was there.

SAINT PETER'S COLLEGE LIBRARY
JERSEY CITY, NEW JERSEY 07306

Rennie was an extremely presentable man, and since he had been backward in forthcomingness she was distinctly piqued. Carlyle, on the other hand, was far too forthcoming, and gave himself away in the most rash manner. He let her know that he had come back from seeing her 'so full of joy that I have done nothing since but dream of it'. And when he sent her the books he even fell into the error of making the lover's cliché : 'It seems as if we had known each other since infancy.' Well might Jane say (on a later occasion) 'I see you don't know how to manage us women.'

When he sent her the books she took a haughty line, merely returning them after reading, with her compliments and addressing her letter to Mr Carslile, a mishandling of his name which she repeated while returning a second batch of books, though he had protested – a curious piece of manners on her part. However, she kept the thing going, got rid of her German tutor, and told Carlyle that on a given Saturday, 'Sir, I will gladly avail myself of your advice.' He replied soberly in terms of a fellow-student, and advised her merely to read Robertson, Hume, Watson, Russell, Voltaire, Tasso, and De Staël in addition to her German studies. Unfortunately, her mother became alarmed at the sight of his letters, and began to make difficulties regarding further meetings, and Jane dared not be caught writing to him.

The agreeable and confidential manner in which she explained this encouraged him to write to her expansively again, and again foolishly. He talked in a lofty and false strain about the Hollowness of Fame, which annoyed her very much, and she roundly declared that she detested a certain letter full of '*meaning* words underlined – meaning sentences half-finished – *meaning blanks* with notes of admiration – and *meaning quotations* from foreign languages'. Furthermore, he had also broken out into *ardent* expressions of friendship. She knocked this with 'One would almost believe the man fancies I have fallen in love with him', and declared, forcibly and falsely, 'I have too *little* romance in my disposition ever to be in love with you or any other man', making herself out as a forbidding blue-stocking.

Yet even after this he wrote again in the wrong strain. He

[*Radio Times Hulton Picture Library*]

Arch House, Ecclefechan. Carlyle's birthplace

Edward Irving (1792-1834). The earliest and 'ever the foremost' of Carlyle's friends.
(Drawn by Robertson)

[*Radio Times Hulton Picture Library*]

Craigenputtock,

[*Radio Times Hulton Picture Library*]

Craigenputtock, Carlyle's house 1828-1834. Jane's inheritance and their Scottish prison

Jane Carlyle (1801-1866) aged 25. After Kenneth Macleary

[*Radio Times Hulton Picture Library*]

referred to himself as 'a perfect wreck', and even wrote, 'Oh for a friend – a bosom friend – the treasure which many seek and few successfully – to be our own and ours alone, to have but one soul and spirit with us, to reflect back our every feeling, to love and be loved without measure!' And still more rash : 'It is cruel and unjust to be angry at what you say, for you mean well.' This was too much for Jane in her present mood. She wrote him a scathing reply, ending with 'You are not my *Friend* – you are not my *Lover*. In the name of wonder, Sir, what *are* you? Oh! I had forgot – A wreck – a perfect wreck! ! ! For heaven's sake Mr Carlyle be, *if you can, a Man* – if not try at least to *seem* one.'

But Carlyle was made of strong material, and did not take mortal offence at this (Irving confessed that such a letter would have finished him off). He lapsed into silence for some weeks, causing her to regret her too haughty expressions, and a month later merely wrote, 'My dear Madam, I happened to fall in with these books lately; and thinking they might perhaps amuse you for a little, I have made bold to send them. You will pardon me for doing so, if it be offensive to you.' He scored. In accepting the books she signed herself, 'Yours with humility'. Thus the way was cleared again on this front for a further advance – or advances, as we call the attentions of a lover. And soon it was 'Yours affectionately'.

Yet, at just about this time, to Jane's surprise, he sank into a state of depression. There were two reasons for this – the state of his stomach, and a religious crisis. The second was about to clear up. The first remained with him all his life, recurrent dyspepsia being a great cause of unhappiness in himself, and an even greater cause of unhappiness in others around him. Never excessively cheerful, this defective interior made him intolerably irritable. Well might he cry, 'What in these days are terrors of conscience to diseases of the liver? Not on morality but on cookery let us build our stronghold.'

He made that remark in his *Sartor Resartus* which he was to write later – though it interferes with his main theme, since good meals do not necessarily promote a good philosophic outlook, nor bad meals a bad one. However in *Sartor Resartus* with superabundant paraphernalia he celebrated his passing from what he called the 'Everlasting No' to the 'Everlasting Yea'. No longer able to rest in the comfort of the Christian scheme of salvation, and under the influence of the new science, the world appeared to him little better than a meaningless machine. 'To me the Universe was all void of Life, of Purpose, of Volition, even of Hostility : it was one huge, dead, immeasurable Steam-engine, rolling on, in its dead indifference, to grind me limb from limb. O, the vast, gloomy, solitary Golgotha, and Mill of Death' etc., etc. (Again, from *Sartor Resartus*.)

He had fallen into a very low mood, and went to Mainhill, where his family were much concerned about him. He wandered about restlessly, unable to eat or sleep or even read. His mother could not bear it, covering him with pious reproaches and lamentations. His father, as usual, let him alone, trusting that he would pull out of it. He did. One day, taking a walk on Leith Hill, his mind suddenly cleared. It was a mystic experience. He beheld a vision of glory. He saw the supernatural in the natural : 'What is Nature? Ha! why do I not name thee God? Art thou not the Living Garment of God? O Heavens, is it, in very deed, HE, then, that ever speaks through thee; that lives and loves in thee, that lives and loves in me?' He surrendered, as did his master, Goethe, 'in awe before the pure phenomena'. Death had seemed terrifying to him : now it was in the circle of life. He never fell from this position. He held to it throughout his life. His faith never failed him, as it failed Tolstoy and Ruskin and Strindberg, and even Wordsworth, in the end. He was a wind-bag in the nineteenth-century manner, and the wind has tended to obscure the solid basis upon which he stood – that of mysticism rather than theology.

6   First Movement in Courtship

THE heady transport of joy which followed upon his period of
religious despondency could not be explained to Jane nor shared
with her. He realized this, and it showed his good sense. Generally,
after any such experience the temptation is to tell everyone about
it excitedly. Carlyle kept it to himself, and left Edinburgh in
August to seek the peace of the countryside, just when Jane
arrived there to enjoy the Capital *en fête* to celebrate the King's
residence there for a fortnight. This behaviour surprised her, for,
if she did not approve of being praised and run after, this did not
mean that she approved of being neglected. However, she decided
to have a good time in Edinburgh with the officers of the garrison
and to play the part of 'a lively, dashing, good-humoured,
thoughtless blockhead of a girl', as she expressed it. This she could
and did do easily enough, it was an inherent part of the early Jane
Welsh. Yet when she received Carlyle's next letter she replied,
'Never did a letter meet a warmer welcome.' She added, 'These
last two months of idleness have done me a deal of mischief. I
cannot study seriously for an hour.' She was impatient for him to
hurry up and show the world what *he* could do – 'Oh if I had
your talents what a different use I would make of them!' And she
required him to write her a long letter.

It is difficult to conceive of Carlyle failing to comply with such
a request – nor did he. The thing for her to do, he said, was to
'attain intellectual eminence'. This could be reached by simply
studying 'whatever great or noble thing men have done or
conceived since the commencement of civilization'. Easy enough,
he declared, if she worked with regularity, beginning with four
hours a day on history. It is not known what she thought of this,
but at about the same time she had an exhortation from Irving
which ran, 'I could wish that your mind was less anxious for the

25

distinction of being enrolled amidst those whom the world hath crowned with their admiration, than amongst those whom God hath crowned with His approval.' She couldn't take this letter, which she described as grotesque. Irving had gone to London and made such a reputation as a preacher that fifteen hundred people struggled to get into his church, and even Royalty attended his sermons. Earlier he had assured Jane that his head would not be turned by success, but that with God's help he would 'rise toweringly aloft into the regions of a very noble and sublime character'. But his head was turned. The flattery was too beguiling. Not a syllable of what he preached has come down to us. We have only Jane's satiric take-off : "Is it not a shame, yea a black and burning shame", to enslave his gigantic powers to such paltry worse than womanish affectations.' Nowadays, we would call such a man phoney. It would not be quite fair : he was an actor. He was a performer, sincerely moving within the mores and faith of the day to make dazzling effects for a term. Anyway, he helped Jane to discern Carlyle more clearly. There was such a difference between the two men : the one with all his goods in the shop-window, the other with hidden depths and fires not yet heaved up. Jane had come to *need* Carlyle now. He had written himself into her life. The pen was his great sword in this enterprise. On the occasions when her spirits flagged, and she felt depressed, his letters made such a difference, she explained to Eliza Stodart '. . . but then comes one of Mr Carlyle's letters that inspires me with new resolution, and brightens all my hopes and prospects.'

Even so, he continued to make psychological mistakes which slowed up his courtship. When she wrote him a very amusing letter about Irving, he put up a show of being distressed and then went on to praise her, extravagantly calling her 'a shining jewel' and speaking of her 'native loveliness' and so on. In consequence, she became condescending again and mocked him with the 'I see that you don't know how to manage us women. You ought above all things beware of seeming grateful for any favour we may please to confer on you.' Yet he failed to take the hint. He tried his hand at a novel with Jane as the heroine, described as 'Think of a slender delicate creature – formed in the very mould of beauty –

elegant and airy in her movements as a fawn; black hair and eyes – jet black; her face meanwhile as pure and fair as lilies – and then for its expression – how shall I describe it? Nothing so changeful, nothing so lovely in all its changes: one moment it was sprightly gaiety, quick arch humour, sharp wrath, the most contemptuous indifference – then all at once there would spread over it a celestial gleam of warm affection, deep enthusiasm . . .' And so on, all without a trace of the original talent which he showed when not under this influence. Yet, strange to say, she did not round on him for this piece.

They could meet very seldom because Jane's mother always contrived to prevent it. But Mrs Welsh now began to relent, and they met again in February 1823. It was a success. Some further meetings were foiled, which infuriated Jane, though Carlyle seemed to take it philosophically. When things were going all right for her and she was made much of and surrounded by admiring suitors and felt well on top, she was condescending enough; but if she was having a bad time with relatives, or not getting her own way, or found Carlyle less floored than he ought to be, she naively fell into self-pity. In short, she was a normal young lady.

As their friendship grew – which meant so much to her – she could not refrain from giving expression to her elation, with the delightful exuberance that was part of her nature. 'Your existence is so identified with all my projects and pursuits that it can only be effaced when I have ceased to feel,' she wrote. 'We shall never forget each other. Our friendship is no paltry intimacy. . . I am persuaded it was planned by Mother Nature. We shall be friends *for ever*.' And presently she wrote these words:

'Oh you have no notion how great a blessing our correspondence is to me! When I am vexed I write my grievances to you; and the assurance I have that your next letter will bring me consolation, already consoles me – and then, when your letter comes, when it repeats to me that *One* in the world loves me – will love me for ever; and tells me more boldly than Hope, that my future *may* yet be glorious and happy;

there is no obstacle I do not feel prepared to meet and conquer. I owe you much! feelings and sentiments that ennoble my character, that give dignity interest and enjoyment to my life – in return, I can only love you, and that I do, from the bottom of my heart.'

Carlyle, now at the age of twenty-eight, did not have enough sagacity to know how to handle this letter – and what sufferable man has this sagacity in his twenties? His best course would have been to enjoy the marvellous glow the letter gave him and yet not reply for a week; then to talk about other things, at the end of the letter simply saying, 'thank you, darling, for your lovely letter'. Thus he would not do the slightest dotting of i's or crossing of t's, giving her leeway for reaction from her unguarded outburst of affection, while at the same time not ignoring it. Instead he instantly seized his pen and wrote, 'Jane loves me! she loves me! and I swear by the immortal powers that she shall be mine, as I am hers, through life and death and all the dark vicissitudes that await us here or hereafter.' And a lot more in the same vein.

Jane Welsh did not love Carlyle, now or ever, with any degree of passion. It was affection she felt, and gratitude for the renewed hope and strength he gave her, and in her elation she could not help rewarding him with 'in return I can only love you.' It was far from a passionate declaration.

She did not receive his reply to that letter for some time, for she had gone somewhere with her mother. When she did get it she was alarmed by what she had done, and scornful of his rash improving of the occasion. What she wrote to him then has often been held against her, regarding both its manner and its matter. But she merely said, in her forthright way, exactly what she felt : 'Is it not true that you regard me, like the bulk of my silly sex, incapable of entertaining a strong affection for a man of my own age without having for its ultimate object our union for life?' She meant it. Hers was not the love, the passion, that longs to get possession of the other person. She loved him, but she was not in love with him, she said – and there certainly is a big difference here. It did not occur to her that there would be any difficulty in getting Carlyle to remain permanently in the wings while giving her all she needed. She went on to say how she had abandoned all womanly prudence and etiquette in saying how she loved and admired his noble qualities, and how she responded to the extraordinary affection he had shown towards her. She continued, 'My Friend I love you – I repeat it tho' I find the expression a rash one – all the best feelings of my nature are concerned in loving you. But were you my Brother I would love you the same, were I married to another I would love you the same... Your Friend I will be, your truest and most devoted Friend, while I breathe the breath of life; but your Wife! never never! Not though you were as rich as Croesus, as honoured and renowned as you yet shall be.'

Carlyle was not always unwise, and, as we have seen, he was good at not taking offence at a hard knock, and at not sulking. Moreover, he had now the insight to discern that while he was more ardent than she, it was he who was the stronger, it was he who was the least dependent. He replied with dignity. He dropped rhetorical flourishes and coolly drew her attention to the fact that he had not mentioned marriage, and said he was not anxious to marry. 'I have no idea of dying in the Arcadian Shepherd's style for the disappointment of hopes which I never seriously entertained, and had no right to entertain seriously.' He was careful to add, in passing, that of course if she married someone else, he would not consider it wise to continue writing to her; and he was not surprised that she then declared that if he stopped writing to her, she would never marry. 'Were the memory of you torn away from me, my whole existence would be laid waste. Oh I do love you my own brother! I even wish that Fate had designed me for your Wife, for I feel that such a destiny is happier than mine is like to be.' Already she was getting the worst of it, which became even more evident in a short time.

☼

7 Second Movement

IRVING married Isabella Martin, and invited Jane and Carlyle to stay with him in London. She was so delighted with the prospect that again she wrote rashly, 'I am almost out of my wits with joy. You and I are going to London! You and I! We are to live a whole summer beside each other.' They were going to have the happiest time 'imagination ever conceived'. They would be always together in occupations and amusements. There would be 'no duties to interfere with the duty of loving each other; no pitiful restraints to vex our happy intercourse'. She concluded, 'I know that the noblest heart in Britain loves me. How comes it that I have such a Friend as you?'

But Carlyle didn't want to go to London. The idea of enjoying himself there and relaxing before he had found his feet seemed to him highly unrealistic. Irving had been tremendously sanguine about his friend's prospects in the capital. He himself had done very well, and he thought that Carlyle would advance in the literary world as fast he did in the preaching line. Carlyle's own assessment of his chances was much more cool. Yes, he thought, 'all seems possible to him; all is joyful and running upon wheels'. He knew that things would not run on wheels for him. 'Irving figured out purposes of unspeakable profit to me, which when strictly examined all melted into empty air. He seemed to think that if set down on London streets some strange development of genius would take place in me, that by conversing with Coleridge and the Opium-eater I should find out new channels for speculation, and soon learn to speak with tongues.'* Carlyle was more sensible

* Carlyle, *Reminiscences* and *Journals*

than most writers in their youth, and did not daydream in this kind. Jane was amazed that he did not want to go. Romantically expecting more from life than it is likely to yield, she thought he would easily make a thousand pounds if he went to London, while also enjoying life with her. Luckily he was not forced into a decision, for Irving was obliged to withdraw his invitation because his just-wed wife put her foot down at the prospect of having the flirtatious Miss Welsh as a guest.

Thus Jane had already come up against a side of Carlyle that should have made her pause, yet it seems to have advanced his suit. Her 'Dearest Friend' became 'Dearly Beloved', and on one occasion when an expected letter did not arrive she was very indignant. 'In the name of heaven why don't you write to me?' she asked. 'You cannot conceive what anxiety I am in about you.' He wrote, and she declared, 'Devil! That I had you here to beat you with a stick! Such a fright you have given me!' In her forthright feminine way she was not devious as a man would have been, but calmly elected to overlook and forget her haughty condescensions of the past. 'I will not write again. Do not urge me lest you wear out my patience and with it my esteem.' That was her tone during Act One. The change did not escape Carlyle.

Though Irving was now unable to invite Jane to stay with them in London he again pressed Carlyle to do so, and at length prevailed upon him to go, and he set off by boat from Scotland. Carlyle had already acquired his gift of what may be described as harshly humorous depiction. Here is a passenger on the boat: 'He had a large long lean head like a sepulchral urn. His face, pock-pitted, hirsute and bristly, was at once vast and hatchet-faced. He stood for many hours together with his left hand laid upon the boat on the middle of the deck, and the thumb of his right hand stuck firmly with its point on the hip joint; his large blue and rheumy eyes gazing on vacancy, the very image of thick-lipped misery. Captain Smith was of quite an opposite species, brisk, lean, whisking, smart of speech. . .' Nearly every word an image.

Presently he was with Edward Irving, and thus describes

him to Jane, as a father – 'Oh that you saw the Giant with his broad-brimmed hat, his sallow visage, and his sable, matted fleece of hair, carrying the little pepper-box of a creature folded in his monstrous palms along the beach, tick ticking to it, and dandling it, and every time it stirs an eyelid grinning horribly a ghastly smile, heedless of the crowds of petrified spectators that turn round in long trains, gazing in silent terror at the fatherly leviathan.' He was brought to see Coleridge, whom he described to his brother John as 'a mass of richest spices putrefied into a dunghill. I never hear him *tawlk* without feeling ready to worship him, and toss him in a blanket. He never straightens his knee-joints. He stoops with his fat, ill-shapen shoulders, and in walking he does not tread, but shovel and slide.' Carlyle could bring to life in a few words those whom he had seen. Later, with the same powerful imagery, he gave astonishing dramatic life to those whom he had not seen – as in *The French Revolution*.

Faced with the London literary world, he was aghast. 'Good heavens! I often inwardly exclaim, and is *this* the Literary World. This rascal rout, this dirty rabble, destitute not only of feeling or knowledge or intellect, but even of common honesty.' For him this was a natural reaction. From his high view-point it was *just*. He could not help being shocked. His standards were above the reach of ordinary men, and he had not realized this, and had not expected what he found. His own superior qualities caused him to despair. Who would want *him*? he wondered. He saw his translation of *Wilhelm Meister* published without any author-optimism. But then, one day, at this very time when he was in London, a knock at his door. Enter a liveried lackey sent round by a certain Lordship in Cavendish Square to deliver – *a letter from Goethe*! Could he believe his eyes? It was like an angel's visitation. Here was the real hand and signature of that mysterious personage whose name had floated through his mind like a spell since his youth, whose thoughts had come to him with the impressiveness of revelations. His spirits rose a good deal at this. His belief in himself, never excessive, was further fortified when later his *Life of Schiller* was published and Goethe spoke of this unknown Scotsman as having the characteristic of a true man of genius, and 'as a new moral force, the extent and effects of which it was impossible to predict'.

Meanwhile Carlyle did meet some people he actually liked. Chief of these were Mrs Strachey and her cousin Kitty Kirkpatrick. They invited him to accompany them to Paris, and he went there for twelve days, taking in the scene with his extraordinary power of observation which served him well when he came to write *The French Revolution*. He wrote to Jane in glowing terms of both Mrs Strachey and Kitty. 'This Kitty is a singular and very pleasing creature; a little black-eyed, auburn-haired brunette, full of kindliness and humour, and who never I believe was angry at any creature for a moment in her life. Tho' twenty-one, and not unbeautiful, the sole mistress of herself and £20,000, she is meek and modest as a Quaker... Would you and I were half as happy as this girl!'

Jane was far from gratified by this, coming from a man who so short a time ago had been 'a perfect wreck' on her account. Having forbidden him, in suitable terms, ever to mention Kitty Kirkpatrick again, she replied in kind. She gave an extremely amusing description of the suitors lined up at her door, one of them collapsing in a faint when she refused him, 'followed by spasms which lasted nearly an hour'. The most presentable was a handsome man of fashion called Captain James Baillie. 'He is my very *beau ideal*', she wrote to Liza Stodart, 'in all respects but one : his nature is the most affectionate I ever knew, his spirit the most magnificent; he has a clear, quick intellect, a lively fancy : with beauty, brilliance, sensibility, native gracefulness, and courtly polish, he wants but *genius* to be – the destiny of my life.' That is a significant instance of her romanticism. Genius she must have, and with it elegance. Not impossible, but not easy to be found. She thought she saw this in Lord Byron, and was wildly taken with him. Shortly after Carlyle had received that letter from Goethe he received one from Byron. Jane was in raptures about it. 'This, then, was *his* handwriting, *his* whose image had haunted my imagination for years and years; whose wild glorious spirit had tinctured all the poetry of my Being! *he*, then, had seen and touched this very paper – I could almost fancy that his look and touch were visible on it!' Presently Byron died. When she heard of it she declared that if she had been told that the sun and moon had gone out, it could not have come to her as a greater shock. Since Carlyle's hero was Goethe, he didn't feel it so keenly, and replied in a too-literary strain of sorrow.

8 *Third Movement*

UNDER the influence of Captain Baillie, Jane now made a mistake. She wrote another of her condescending letters, and suggested that after having travelled Carlyle should have dropped his Annandale accent and appear more polished. She told him that it was time that he made more progress with his pen and used to advantage the favourable contacts he had made in London. This frightened him. He knew he would never advance in this manner, that way being reserved for what Keats called the regiment of 'the little famous', and that nothing but a slow grind would see him through. Indeed, he was doubtful of getting through. Perhaps it was hopeless relying upon literature to support him, and it would be better to help one of his brothers at farming and write in his spare time. Jane was horrified. If that's what he wanted, she said mockingly, why not improve her piece of land at Craigenputtock? He took this seriously. Why not? he asked. He would be ready to go there as soon as possible, and when everything was ship-shape he would invite her to join him there.

She was appalled. And now a series of immensely long letters passed between them. She poured scorn on this Craigenputtock idea. He continued to regard it as excellent, thinking only of himself. She said that she didn't love him well enough to make such a sacrifice. Then she discovered that he didn't love her well enough to sacrifice what he thought would alone give him health and sanity. Both were wise in their self-regard. This was a truthful moment: it was the moment when they should have parted for ever. He was ready to do so. He said so. She could not do it. She could not break from him. She could not stick to her guns; 'your spirit has gained such a mastery over mine, in spite of my pride and stubborness'. She climbed down and temporized. Inconsistent with all she had said before, she wrote, 'How could I part from the only living soul that understands me? I would marry you tomorrow rather; our parting would need to be brought about by death or some dispensation of Providence.' This was an illusion. She was admirably suited to be the wife of a successful and cultivated statesman – but not a writer like Carlyle. He had no need of a wife – only someone to look after him, as the strange phrase goes. He was under-sexed. He had no desire for children : throughout all his works his only reference to babies is in terms of derision. Some women, having 'got their man', neglect him after the family is born. Some men whose only children are works of art, neglect their wives in the same way.

Unquestionably, this was the moment when the truth could be seen by those who had eyes to see. It was clear to Mrs Welsh : it was hidden from Jane, and largely from Carlyle. The main truth about marriage is concealed from lovers because it cannot be experienced beforehand or even conceived by them – the daily grind in terms of self-interest. When an ordinary man and woman decide on marriage the step is remarkable enough. Two people who don't know each other to any extent (they cannot!) invite each other to all meals, and to bed, and to house, for the rest of their lives. It sounds crazy. It often works. Even so it is an extraordinary venture, no matter how often or universally done. If one of the couple is a genius, an additional hazard of uncertain and possibly appalling pro-portions is present. If both of them are a genius it is worse. If one of them is a bit of a genius and the other full scale it is worse still. Here, you would think, kind friends will have to rush to the rescue and avoid the disaster. But they are pow-erless. The relations and friends of Jane Welsh and Carlyle could do nothing to prevent the net closing upon them.

Carlyle was a literary genius in the full scale. And what is that which marks the man out from others who may write just as well or better? It is a certain passion in him. It declares itself in his style, good or bad, giving it a harmony, a music that we recognize. He has an angle of approach all his own – no one.

else slants his pen in that way. He has taken up a position. He rests on a foundation. He sees something from afar. He hears something, perhaps the veritable Voice of the Universe, and somehow we know that he hears it. He is possessed by a spirit of missionary zeal foreign to others however talented. His mission is his first consideration. He must not spare himself. He does not spare others who appear to interfere with his work. This is selfishness on a scale other than that of greed or petty self-regard. An embattled figure, obsessed with some great purpose, not even clear to himself, he does not belong to the ordinary run of men and stands apart. This gives him authority. It gives him force. In the urgency of his energy a great wind blows from him, and in the storm of his mind his words become streaming ensigns and tossing branches. So it was with Carlyle. Jane saw it. She responded to it. She could not fail to be borne along on that wind, drawn to that light, and warmed by that fire. Yet again it was romantic of her. For *his* definition of genius was 'an infinite capacity for taking pains'. She had not reckoned with the pains, whether for him or for herself. In the event, no greater pains were ever experienced by a writer, or by the wife of a writer.

After the exchange of letters about Craigenputtock, Carlyle spent such a happy time that it boded ill for the future. He had an exceptionally strong constitution. This is hardly in question, seeing the amount he rode on horseback in all weathers, and the enormous output of immense letters he wrote, in addition to his massive volumes of history – only a very strong man could have possibly conducted such operations. But his dyspepsia was real enough, and the 'bad health' he persistently complained of, though largely imaginary, was real to himself, and this told on his nerves. Determined to get back his health, as he put it, after his return from London, he went to a farmhouse at Hoddam Hill which his doting family found for him near their place.

He was exceedingly content there, and it was perhaps the only period during the course of his life when he acknowledged that he was happy. He was at peace. He wasn't bothered by anything or anybody. He could do exactly what he liked – ride out in the glorious countryside or work. He had enough money in hand coming in from the periodicals to free him from present worry. One of his sisters and his mother kept house and cooked for him; no trouble ever taxed their devotion to 'dear Tom'. 'If I choose to dine on fire and brimstone they will cook it for me with their best skill', he told Jane. Here his stomach did not pull him down, and his spirit was raised up. He consolidated the victory he had won earlier by his mystical experience. His mood was Wordsworthian, and if his best work is poor in comparison with the greatest of British poets, it is nevertheless lasting. 'There is a majesty and mystery in nature, take her as you will,' he wrote from Hoddam. 'Is she not immovable, eternal and immense in Annandale as she is in Chamounie? The chambers of the East are opened in every land, and the sun comes forth to sow the earth with orient pearl. Night, the ancient mother, follows him with her diadem of stars; and Arcturus and Orion call *me* into the Infinitudes of space as they called the Druid priest or the shepherd of Chaldea. Bright creatures! how they gleam like spirits through the shadows of innumerable ages from their thrones in the boundless depths of heaven.' This was no passing lyric ecstasy. He had said farewell to argument in religious terms and could rest in peace.

Jane, who had little interest in his recent mysticism, became far from pleased at his present courtship. 'I have never been so idle or so happy', he wrote to her, which was not what she wished to hear, especially as she was idle and unhappy. 'I am heartily sick of my existence in this miserable Haddington,' she complained. Something had to be done. At this point an interfering third person served her purpose.

A mutual friend called Mrs Montagu, who knew that Jane had once loved Edward Irving, on learning that Carlyle was contemplating marrying her, at once took action. Such a match would never do, she decided, quite sensibly; but then, with neither sense nor sensibility, and with almost superfeminine ambiguity of phrase, wrote to both of them. Carlyle didn't grasp what she was telling him, for he did not know up to this time that Jane had loved Irving, as she had kept it from him and later could not refrain from mocking at the preacher's ludicrous antics. Carlyle was bewildered by Mrs Montagu's letter to him, but Jane saw that this was an opportunity to get him into a more urgent state of mind. A curious episode followed. She had once loved Irving: she had kept it to herself. That was all. So what? – anyone might fairly ask, even in the nineteenth century. But she whipped it up. She wrote to Carlyle in an hysterical strain, revealing the 'secret' and throwing herself upon his mercy for the 'deception' in a manner worthy of Act III in a melodrama.

The letter failed to reach him at once, and fearing that she had overdone it, she wrote again. 'Mr Carlyle do you mean to kill me? Is it just of you to keep me so long in doubt? Your displeasure I have merited, perhaps your scorn, but surely not this terrible silence. Write then for Heaven's sake! and kindly, if you can, for I am wretched beyond all expression. Had I but strength I would come to you this very day, and when I held you in my arms and you saw my tears you would forget everything but the love I bear you.' He replied in strains of lofty and humble sentiment suitable to the occasion, but her terms had served to alarm him. He made another bid for freedom. Was it too late to call it off? Writing in a style far too rhetorical, he rehearsed the flaws in his character and his incapacity for happiness. 'My heart has been steeped in solitary bitterness ... Am I not poor and sick and helpless and estranged from all men? I lie upon the thorny couch of pain, my pillow is the iron pillow of despair: I can rest on them in silence, but that is all that I can do. Think of it, Jane! I can never make you happy. Leave me, then! Why should I destroy you? It is but one bold step and it is done.' Written in that manner, Jane could not see, or would not see, the red light. She became still more agitated and fervent. 'Leave you! Obey the voice of reason! You know not what you say! ...'

He could not resist this appeal. 'We may still be happy,' he declared. At this she at once took another step and paid a visit to his mother and family. Carlyle had always been nervous about such a meeting, because of their disparity of class. Jane had no such fear. She knew she could take it in her stride. She did so.

Like all well-bred people she made class-difference vanish, and captivated the whole family; while her subsequent letters to Mrs Carlyle are wonderful in the simple psychology with which she realized that the proper way to write was in her normal clever sophisticated literary manner, the whole informed with a charming and sincere affection. Her conquest was complete.

There remained only the obstacle of her own mother. Mrs Welsh clung to her with passionate possession. Jane was afraid to cross her : the mother's tongue was strong and swift but met its match in the daughter, whom she found somewhat of a shrew. Yet their mutual devotion was deep. The proof of this was made manifest by an unusual action on Jane's part. There is nothing so sincere as a money transaction. As we have seen, Jane was an heiress, inheriting the estate of Craigenputtock and certain investments. She now made it all over to her mother. Her motives were love and a momentary satisfaction of Power – momentary, for she thereby burnt her financial boats and would be henceforth at the mercy of a husband's purse. It was a rare and remarkable thing to do.

The next thing was to get her mother to accept Carlyle as a son-in-law. This was difficult, for Mrs Welsh clearly saw how mother-spoilt and sister-spoilt and brother-spoilt Carlyle was, making him likely to be a most selfish husband. She had seen him as moody, violent, and imperious. He had displayed extremely bad temper even in front of her. But when she found that Jane was determined on this alliance and suddenly proposed that her mother would live with them and not be abandoned, she burst into tears and cried, 'Why have you never said as much before?' Unfortunately this did no good, for when Carlyle was told, he rejected it outright. He must rule in the house, he insisted; imagine Mrs Welsh being ruled by him, imagine her taking him as guardian and director and 'being a second wife to her daughter's husband!' Yet, though he would not (wisely) have Mrs Welsh living with them, he suggested that Jane come and live with *his* family at Scotsbrig. He thought of himself only; not of Jane, or of his family, who did not favour so rash a scheme.

Presently Mrs Welsh decided to give up the house at Haddington and go to live at Templand with her father. Then Carlyle surpassed himself. Here was an unexpected piece of good luck, he intimated; if she is going to give up the excellent residence, let us go there and take her place! He was too insensitive to see how much this would embarrass Jane at a house where everyone in her social circle would consider that she had married beneath her to an eccentric farmer's son with no prospects. He told her that he would make short work of unwelcome visitors (unwelcome to him). 'The moment I am master of a house,' he said, 'the first use I turn it to will be to slam the door of it in the face of nauseous intrusions of all sorts.' These intruders were the companions who had grown up with Jane for twenty years.

Could she not now see the signs and retire before it was too late? Apparently not. Just now she could only take his great qualities seriously – qualities she wanted in a husband, without counting what might be their price in wretchedness and loneliness. She saw the elegant Captain Baillie again, now in her eyes only 'a fine gentleman,' nothing compared with 'the *man* I love.' There was no self-deception about this: 'Strange as you may think it, young man, I have an affection for thee which it is not in the power of language to express.' Nevertheless, she wrote jestingly that perhaps it wouldn't be a bad thing if they did go their separate ways. Why not let him take Miss Kitty Kirkpatrick with her £20,000 and agreeable character, and she take one of the many eligible men longing to have her? – but she ended with the cry, 'What's the use, we are married already, married past redemption.' This did no good. He elected to take it seriously, and unchivalrously replied that they were *not* married already, that he agreed with her that she could make a much better match than with him, indeed that 'it would be a piece of news for me to learn that I am not the very worst you ever thought of.' He realized also that she was not seeing him clearly: 'It is not the poor, unknown, rejected Thomas Carlyle that you know, but the prospective rich, known, and admired.' That was true. It was natural in her. And it made him afraid. Greater love

41

hath no man than this, he might have said, than that he lay down his life – for his work. He would win through somehow, someway, if he had to live on a few pence (why not? he asked), but he would not, and saw that he could not, pot-boil to any extent. He would not lay down his work for a wife. Again he made his bid for freedom. 'If you judge fit, I will take you to my heart as my wedded wife this very week. If you judge it fit, I will this very week forswear you for ever.' But again she would not have it. She would not face the reality. She would not turn aside from her dream. 'If you love me, cease, I beseech you, to make me offers of freedom; for this is an outrage which I find it not easy to forgive.'

At this point – in one of the strangest, and, in retrospect, saddest, courtships in history – Mrs Welsh herself decided to solve their house problem. She sold the place at Haddington for a handsome sum. At one stroke she had made certain that Carlyle could not take over Haddington, and at the same time, with money in hand over and above what Jane had handed over to her, she could find a house for them in Edinburgh. Mother and daughter went there and took a pleasant place at 21 Comely Bank. They set to work to make it into a really comfortable home. They were both in high spirits, for now the Mrs Welsh problem would be solved, since without living in the same house she would be near her daughter.

The rest followed inexorably. But the lovers now became nervous. Indeed as the wedding-day drew near they both became as frightened as if they were going to execution. Carlyle fell into a low state. 'I look forward to this affair', he wrote to his brother John, 'with very *queer* feelings.' His dyspepsia came on in full force and he felt 'splenetic, sick, sleepless, void of faith, hope, and charity'. He hoped he would pull out of this, other-wise 'a certain incident will wear a quite original aspect', he said to Jane. She replied that if he didn't face the squad better '*the* incident will not only wear a very original aspect, but likewise a very heartbreaking one'. She declared that the coming ceremony was odious to her; that she didn't see how she could go through with it, and that she turned quite sick at the thought. He tried to cheer himself up by reading Kant's *Critique of Pure Reason*. She turned to the poems of Byron. But neither reason nor romance served to elevate their drooping spirits. They attempted to console one another. He implored her not to take it too much to heart: 'Have not many people been married before?' He swore it would break his heart if he made her unhappy. And she, 'Oh my dearest friend! be always so good to me and I shall make the best and happiest Wife!', though she added that when at times he fled from her caresses to smoke or speak of her as a new *circumstance* of his lot, she was filled with anxiety. To this he replied that he would think his life well spent if he could make hers happy. On the day before the wedding (October 1826) details of procedure were drawn up, headed 'The last Speech and marrying Words of that unfortunate young woman, Jane Baillie Welsh', a bulletin which Carlyle declared to be 'worthy of such a maiden bidding farewell to the unmarried earth of which she was the fairest ornament'.

✵

9   Hopes at Comely Bank

THE ceremony over, they settled down at Comely Bank. Jane
adapted well. She had a clear job in front of her, the
running of the first home of her own with a husband to look
after. Whatever she did, she did thoroughly, whether flirting
and having a good time, or, as now, subordinating herself
for the sake of one man. She was happy in this, and
hopeful. But it is clear from the guarded way in which she
told his mother that 'we are really very happy; and when he
falls upon some work we shall be still happier', that all was
not well with him. She had no complaints regarding his
treatment of her: 'My husband is so kind! so, in all respects
after my own heart! I was sick one day, and he nursed me
as well as my own Mother could have done, and he never
says a hard word to me – unless I richly deserve it.' But she
said he had fallen into a low mood, a very Slough of
Despond.

Carlyle had no fault to find with her. She is the best of
all wives, he told his mother 'I am astonished at the
affection she bears me, and the patience with which she
listens to my doleful forebodings and turns them all into gay
hopes'. He was far from hopeful about the future, for he
was not yet sure of his next literary move. His stomach
always gave him extra trouble when his work was going
badly, and his dyspepsia now returned in full force. 'My
husband's particular friends – the Destinies, *alias* the Upper
Powers, *alias* the Immortal Gods', as Jane Carlyle put it at a
much later date, were expected to keep an eye on him.
Sometimes, however, he was more inclined to call to his aid
cooks and chemists. Virtue is its own reward, he admitted,
but only in the sense that a good nervous system – regardless

44

of the state of one's conscience – is its own reward. 'What follows then? Pay off your moralist, and hire two apothecaries and two cooks. Socrates is inferior to Captain Barclay; and the *Enchiridion* of Epictetus must hide its head before Kitchener's Peptic Receipts. Heed not the immortality of the soul so long as you have beefsteaks, porter, and – blue pills' – as he later phrased it in *Sartor Resartus*. But the potion which he needed most at the moment was not a pill so much as a good literary plan.

He made the mistake of attempting a novel, and was now obliged to abandon it. Carlyle had no *invention*, says Froude truly. He had a powerful imagination. It is possible to have both, of course; but the distinction is important. Imagination is the power to see what is there. Invention is the power to see what is not there – and so is fancy. Imagination allows a man to see a tree in all its pristine mysteriousness: fancy may see fairies in its branches. Imagination is the concentration of feeling and seeing and thinking all at the same pitch at once – it is 'Reason in her most exalted mood', as Wordsworth put it. The explanation why *Moby Dick* has sometimes been called the greatest novel ever written is because of its imaginative power. The mighty Melville had laid hold of the facts: he had thrust his hand into the waters and held up Leviathan for all men to see for evermore. Carlyle loved to lay hold of facts. The time was to come when he too would lift them up to shine in epic form. But that time was not yet.

He had not yet made himself felt as a literary figure, but he was already famous as a talker. Jane made a surprising remark to his mother at this time. She declared that she had no gift for talking. One had thought otherwise: it had seemed she was not entirely tongue-tied. But now she says, 'often when Carlyle has talked for an hour without answer he will beg for some sign of life on my part, and the only sign I can give him is a little kiss'. And even he mentions how she sits 'mum'. No doubt he induced mumness, if not numbness. He was to become celebrated as the most remarkable talker of the century, with only Macaulay as runner-up. He was never a bore, for his massive knowledge in so many surprising directions, allied with an exceptional memory, promoted the particular instance, which is the core of good talk, while his wild exaggerations, his extraordinary metaphors and frequent flashes of humour, always held attention – it was the chief spell that had won him his wife. Yet he was always preaching the great virtue of silence. 'His love of silence', said Jane Carlyle in a famous quip, 'was purely Platonic'. But I am sure G. K. Chesterton was right in saying that 'in spite of his praise of silence, it was only through his gift of utterance that he escaped madness'. With such a gift for speech, he did not 'shut the door on intruders' at Comely Bank as he had threatened. They held 'Wednesday Evenings', when many visitors came, and he began his reign as monologue-monarch, from which throne he was never deposed nor sought to abdicate till the end of his life. The main works of this author were not yet written; he was unauthorized; yet since he spoke as one having authority a subsequent fame was already assumed.

These Wednesday evening 'at homes' brought them the friendship of Jeffrey, the then celebrated Editor of the *Edinburgh Review*. He had ignored contributions Carlyle had previously submitted, but on meeting him and Jane he became interested and helpful. He took him into his paper, and the success of his contributions there opened the way for articles in the other learned magazines of the period. Jeffrey was a little man full of life and sparkle and mimicry, a very entertaining companion, of whom they both became fond. He went further in his attempt to help Carlyle by sponsoring him for a post that would relieve him of the necessity of relying on his pen for funds. The post of Professorship for St Andrews University fell vacant, and Jeffrey put Carlyle's name forward, supported by other important signatures, including that of Goethe. Such testimonials as were offered on this occasion were perhaps never before presented by any candidate for a Scottish professorship. But it was in vain. 'It went to Mr Someonelse. The certificate of the angel Gabriel would not have availed, as Froude put it to me, a pin's worth', said Carlyle, truly. It was not in the nature of things that he would have got it. He was too much of an 'original'. He could not be saved in this way. And he would not be saved in a personal way. Jeffrey offered to pay him £100 a year, but he would not take it. The offer was very delicately put, and, indeed, as delicately declined. There was no need to decline it. Carlyle knew how to give, but not how to receive. It caused him great pain to receive a gift of money. Mrs Welsh tried it. Mrs Montagu tried it. And now Jeffrey. Yet, during this period, he was always giving his brother John financial aid, and later Alick as well. He felt it a duty to regard a brother's need as his own. However hard up he was himself, he always managed to send something to John, who was studying to become a doctor. His wife may not have been pleased to go short for the sake of the brothers, but she made no complaint though it meant the end of life at Comely Bank. Even while he was refusing money from Jeffrey he was unable to meet the financial demands of their establishment, and once again he longingly looked towards Craigenputtock as a haven.

When the idea of living there had been put to Jane previously she had declared that she couldn't live at the place for a fortnight with an angel. But now she suggested that he go there to investigate possibilities. After all, her father had been born there and it was her own ancestral property; and her mother approved the scheme, for the house at Templand was not more than a morning's ride from Craigenputtock. Carlyle set out, and was able to negotiate possession of the house in three months' time. So, after two years, the pleasant social scene in Edinburgh was exchanged for one of the loneliest and dullest places in Scotland. 'To her it was a great sacrifice, if to me it was the reverse', he was to write in the years to come. 'But at no moment, even by a look, did she ever say so. Indeed I think she never felt so at all. She would have gone to Nova Zembla with me, and found *it* the right place had benefit to me or set purpose of mine lain there.' We need not think that he exaggerated her devotion, for their feelings for one another are displayed in the letters they exchanged when he had gone over to see about Craigenputtock. 'Not unlike what the drop of water from Lazarus's finger might have been to Dives in the flame was my dearest Goody's letter to her husband yesterday afternoon', he wrote from there. 'Oh Jeannie! oh my wife! we will never part, never through eternity itself; but I will love thee and keep thee in my heart of hearts!' And in the course of her letter she wrote, 'To be separated from you for one week is frightful as a foretaste of what it *might* be... Is not my being interwoven with yours so close that it can have no separate existence? Yes, surely, we will live together and die together and be together through all eternity'.

We are told by his great and devoted biographer, Froude, that Carlyle was unable to consummate his marriage. He was a virgin, and on the wedding-night had found that he was unable to perform. The appalling frustration of this caused him next morning to tear to pieces the flower garden at Comely Bank in a fit of ungovernable fury. Froude was given this information by Jane's most intimate friend and confidante, Geraldine Jewsbury, in circumstances when 'it is entirely inconceivable that she would have uttered any light or ill-considered gossip'. There is no reason to doubt her word. Yet is not such a fact rather incompatible with the tone of these letters, and those written to his mother? It would seem so. Yet two things should be considered. First, the impotence could have been only temporary (as often happens), or there may have been at least partial success to follow, and an understanding compromise of some sort. Second, though the period is only last century, the distance from us is fantastic, especially concerning three things – transport, theological belief, and the attitude towards sex. In our day a woman in Jane's position would feel – certainly the age would compel her to think that she felt – unbearably outraged and deprived. Many women in any age would feel this. But not necessarily all, without prompting by the spirit of the time. In those days it wasn't all a question of terrible suppression; there was also ignorance of bliss. It is possible that the present-day obsession with sex may cause a vast amount of disgruntlement which would not otherwise prey upon us to the same extent.*

---

* See Appendix on the Froude Controversy. So much has been written about this charge of impotence that it cannot be passed over. But to make no mention of it in the text, and only an *ex cathedra* commentary in a Note at the end, as is generally done, and as it is a temptation to do, seems to me utterly inadmissible from a biographical point of view. If there is something – however controversial – which cannot be evaded, it should be set down briefly in the proper chronological position, and not suddenly produced for the reader after the portrait has been finished.

✖

10   *Despair at Craigenputtock*

THE farmstead of Craigenputtock was run by Carlyle's brother
Alick, who occupied one part of the building at first. There were
no other friends within reach. This was Jane's exchange from
presiding over a delightful circle in Edinburgh. The two preced-
ing wives who had been in residence there had not cared for it
much, the first having taken to drink, the second having gone
mad. But a superior person knows that everything depends upon
the significance he gives to the things he has to do. We are really
magicians with power to *make different* anything we do by
changing the meaning of what we do. This is philosophically
obvious, and in practice easy – but seldom extended to include
'menial' tasks. Jane Welsh Carlyle realized this. Indeed, it
suddenly came to her as a revelation. One day she was baking
bread and feeling sorry for herself. Here she was, sixteen miles
away 'in a peat bog' from all conveniences of life, with a sense of
forlornness and degradation. She, who had always been petted
and asked to do nothing but *cultivate her mind*, now had to
watch a loaf of bread – it was too bad, and she sobbed aloud.
Then she thought of Benvenuto Cellini. He had sat up all night
watching his Perseus in the furnace. And the thought came to
her : 'After all, in the sight of the Upper Powers, what is the
mighty difference between a statue of Perseus and a loaf of
bread, so that each be the thing one's hand has found to do?
The man's determined will, his energy, his patience, his resource,
were the really admirable things, of which his statue of Perseus
was the mere chance expression. If he had been a woman living
at Craigenputtock, with a dyspeptic husband, sixteen miles from
a baker, and he a bad one, all the same qualities would have
come out more fitly in a *good* loaf of bread.' This was no passing
thought, it took root in her during those years in 'that savage

place'. Well might she write to a friend, when recounting this thirty years later, that many lives are split and spoiled for failing to recognize that it is not the greatness or the littleness of the task 'but the spirit in which one does it, that makes one's doing noble or mean. I can't think how people who have any natural ambition or any sense of power in them escape going *mad* in a world like this without the recognition of that.'

In this mood she took everything in her stride and, since the Carlylean stomach required fresh milk she learnt to milk cows when occasion demanded. Though never without a servant, she set an example in blacking grates and scouring floors; and when the Jeffreys paid an unexpected visit one day when she was short of stores, she thought nothing of riding to Dumfries and back – some thirty miles – and subsequently entertaining them with a description of her adventures on the way. She was full of energy, believing in Carlyle, believing in the future.

He was not in an equally positive mood. In fact he began to despair of winning his literary battle. In spite of all that Jeffrey could do, there was nothing steady or permanent in writing for periodicals. Jeffrey had resigned his editorship of the *Edinburgh Review* to become Lord Advocate and hoped that possibly Carlyle might succeed him in the Chair (what a tribute that was!). But Carlyle got in the way himself. In vain did Jeffrey plead with him to be less deadly earnest, to ease up a bit, to try and enjoy himself, to recognize the importance of simply being happy and making so remarkable a wife happy. In vain did he appeal to him to eschew 'the desperate darkness of audacious mysticism'. Jeffrey was a good and wise man. Carlyle knew this, but could not mend his ways. He could not be prudent, he made no claim to be good, he took a modest view of his literary powers, but he must be faithful to the Voice. He became subject to deep despondency. Had he lost the way? Would being true to himself just land him in the ditch? He looked up into the empty heavens and saw no sign. Thoughts fall on us, he said, like seed Time and silence alone can ripen them. Being compelled to write for a living destroys them. Yet he could not leave literature. If he had but two potatoes in the world, he declared, and one true idea, it would be his duty to part with one potato to buy paper and ink, and live on the other till he expressed the idea.

In this mood he wrote *Sartor Resartus*. This was, in place of his abandoned novel, to be his bid for popularity with a larger public than that interested in his essays and translations. It would be hard to conceive of a less promising effort to reach a wide public. It was a satiric, philosophical, humorous, part-autobiographical commentary on the shams of life, a simple theme made to appear vastly complex, with some glorious passages, a profound account of turning from Rejection to Acceptance, a number of prophetic, biblical animadversions, the whole founded on the necessity of Wonder. It was put forward as the life and views, in long labyrinthine quotations, of a German professor with the winning name of Teufelsdröckh. Not a book that anyone at any time could easily read through : impossible as a popular book. Yet that is what he wrote. He could do nothing with it from Scotland. In the end he thought that the only thing to do was to go to London and get in touch with publishers there. Surprisingly, he pocketed his pride, accepting £50 as a loan from Jeffrey, and set out. Jane was horrified at being left alone at Craigenputtock. Thirty-four years later the memory of their sad last evening was fresh and plaintive to him.

✖

11 A Sojourn in London

THUS, in August 1831, he set out by boat again, embarking 'amidst bellowing and tumult and fiddling unutterable, all like a spectral vision', as if he were venturing out through regions of shade and night into the vast unknown. However, he arrived safe and sound in London and stayed with his brother John in the house of Edward Irving's brother at Woburn Square.

He was unable to get a letter posted to Jane for a week, and she became feverishly anxious, but was then rewarded with a series of very tender letters. Opening his box so carefully packed by her, he had been quite overcome : 'Heaven reward thee, my clear-headed, warm-hearted, dearest little Screamikin.' And later, 'My love for you does not depend upon looks, and defies old age and decay, and, I can prophesy, will grow stronger the longer we live and toil together'.

Once again he surveyed the London scene. The rich he described as 'gigmen' given over to 'gigmanity', while the Bohemians were, more simply, 'vermin'. Had he only indulged in such large generalizations, the world would not have paid much attention to him; but he carried with him that wonderful lens to snap the particular – so that today, for instance, even those who know little of Robespierre or the French Revolution have heard of the 'sea-green incorruptible'. In his letters at this time he sent back quick little word-sketches of various dignitaries. 'Figure to yourself', he writes of a certain Bowring, otherwise unknown to history, 'a thin man about my height and bent at the *middle* into an angle of 150°, the *back* straight, with large grey eyes, a huge turn-up nose with straight nostrils to the very point, and large projecting close-shut mouth . . .' It seems that he held as firmly as Dickens that the exterior man faithfully reflected the interior. He saw the current Lord Chancellor in the House of Lords :

'The Chancellor is a very particularly ignoble-looking man . . . *nothing* but business in his face . . . he was yawning awfully, with an occasional twitching up of the corners of the upper lip and point of the nose. A politician truly and *nothing* more'. Always a picture, even a moving picture. On Fonblanque, an editor, whom we may rescue from the shades: 'A tall, loose, lank-haired, wrinkly, wintry, vehement-looking flail of a man'. On Sir James Mackintosh: 'A broadish, middle-sized, grey-headed man, and with a plain courteous bearing; grey intelligent (unhealthy yellow-whited) eyes, in which plays a dash of cautious vivacity (uncertain whether fear or latent ire), triangular un-meaning nose, business mouth and chin . . .'

Meanwhile he was having a very bad time in his endeavour to find a publisher for *Sartor Resartus*. Jeffrey had given him a good introduction to the famous House of Murray, who published Byron. Murray rejected the book – after having first accepted it! When it was already in the printer's hands he changed his mind, and returned the manuscript with a trumpery excuse. This action was shamefully handled by the publisher. Carlyle, who was always whining about small things, took big things in his stride. He made no attempt to hold Murray to the contract. Keeping a copy of his letter for posterity, he replied with a courteous dignity and in a spirit as noble and brave as that of Bernard Shaw when for a long time he also was knocking at the door.

This initial failure to procure a publisher for *Sartor* was the prelude to total failure elsewhere. Nevertheless, a good thing happened at the same time. Jeffrey had been able to help his brother John by introducing him to Lady Clare, a rich woman who needed a travelling doctor, a post which carried a salary of £300 a year. He accepted this, and soon would be able to pay back Thomas what he had borrowed. Caryle hastened to tell the good news to Jane and to suggest that she join him in London for the winter. She was delighted. It was too lonely at Craigenputtock, but when she went to her mother at Templand they had rows, and she became sullen and miserable. She had been almost tempted to accept an offer of financial aid from Mrs

5 Cheyne Row. Rented in 1834 and 'where they lived as headquarters for the remainder of their lives'

[Radio Times Hulton Picture Library]

Carlyle and the dog Nero in the back court at 5 Cheyne Row. 1857

[Radio Times Hulton Picture Library]

[*Radio Times Hulton Picture Library*]
John Sterling. Scottish philosopher and writer about whom Carlyle wrote a book in 1850

John Tyndall (1820-1893). Natural Philosopher. He loved Carlyle and looked after him on his trip to receive the Rectorship of the University of Edinburgh
[*Radio Times Hulton Picture Library*]

Montagu to go to London, but finally rejected it as a shocking effrontery. Now she could go without outside assistance. She set out at the end of September, just in time, it seems, to avoid a nervous breakdown caused by her own flurries and her mother's agitations.

She arrived in such a state of headache and collapse that she could eat nothing and took to bed for two days. There was something fundamentally weak about Jane Carlyle's constitution. She caught colds terribly often and easily, and was subject to headache and sickness to an extreme degree. This is a main fact concerning her. Life with Carlyle was to weaken her much more, but he was not the root cause in the first place, and her constant illnesses made an extra burden for him to contend with throughout the years. His brother John, near the end, once lost patience with her, and said cruel and abominable things at an incredibly inappropriate time. Carlyle seldom realized how ill she was, for she concealed the worst from him most of the time; but when he did know, no one could have been more tender.

When she got well, she began to enjoy London life very much. She didn't care a button about 'sights'; she delighted in good company and good talk, and that is what she got. A scarcely known potential writer from Scotland would not normally know anyone, but Carlyle did draw interesting people to him like a magnet, and, in any case, Jeffrey, now living in London, and Charles Buller, already a distinguished and brilliant person, brought people along. Once again they held evening 'at-homes' when Carlyle occupied that little hiding-place of his, the centre of the stage, holding everyone spellbound by his talk, while his great laugh could be heard right down the street. Not everyone met with their approval; indeed it was not easy to obtain the approval of the Carlyles. But they both soon became fond of Leigh Hunt, in spite of the fact that he was grossly over-familied, and of John Stuart Mill. They saw Edward Irving of course, but were very uneasy about the way he was now surrounded with frantic followers 'speaking with tongues'. He was rapidly going down. Pressed on by a deluded wife, he mistook raving women and ranting men for vehicles of the Holy Ghost, and

3—TC * *

histrionic hysterics for prophecy. Attending one of his gatherings Carlyle was constrained to note that 'nothing so shocking and altogether unspeakably deplorable was it ever my lot to hear'. Jane was so upset by the horrible sounds issuing from the lips of a frenzied fanatic, that she cried all the way home and did not recover till breakfast next day. Carlyle was sincerely concerned for his 'high-aspiring, noble-hearted friend'. One evening, in the presence of Jane, he spoke to him non-stop for half an hour, warning him against these theatrical displays and questioning the sense of his rhetorical flourishes and maudlin sermons. Irving was shamed. He averted his gaze, bent low his head, and said not a word. But he could not pause in his Bedlam course. He was beyond the reach of reason or friendly reins, and could not be deflected from self-destruction.

Carlyle was enjoying this London visit almost as much as Jane, and even admitted that 'amid the mass of Stupidity and Falsehood there *is* actually some reasonable conversation to be come at'. He was encouraged by the respect in which he found himself held to believe in his stars, and to think that he might not fail in his mission. By making personal contact with the editors of the literary and political reviews he had plenty of work in hand, and he quite forgot about his stomach. It would have seemed a sound policy to remain in London. But he wavered. Throughout his life he wavered and wandered. He was always restless after a time, wherever he might be. Since they had no definite residence in London and all their belongings were in Scotland, he was in no hurry to burn his boats and risk so drastic a venture as attempting to make the capital his headquarters. *Sartor Resartus* was still being rejected, and he was undecided as to the nature of his next book.

A sudden event then caused him to make up his mind to return to Craigenputtock. On 22 January, 1832, news came from Scotland that his father, James Carlyle, had died. As it was essential that he should finish a commissioned essay on Dr Johnson before leaving, Carlyle stayed on for another two months. But he did immediately write a portrait of his father which is one of the finest of the 'Memoirs' in his *Reminiscences*, and also sent long homilies on death to members of his family. His sister Margaret had died two years earlier and he wrote a fine threnody on her also. It was indeed a remarkable family, and the death of a member was regarded as a ship going down, and the rest as 'survivors'. Carlyle was extremely ostentatious in his grief, requiring to be consoled as if he were an infant, and making everyone around him as uncomfortable as possible, which a man more thoughtful for others would never do. Still, his feeling was deep, for he approved of his father in about the same degree as Ruskin disapproved of his. He held that James Carlyle had as fine an intellect as Robert Burns; and he not only took from him integrity as an inflexible value, and justice and truth as the basis for conduct, but inherited in his literary effects (supposed to be influenced by German writers) his father's method of speech.

✿

12   *The Retreat to Craigenputtock*

THIS retreat from London was a blow for Jane. She had endured one spell at Craigenputtock, and dreaded a second. It took the heart out of her. 'With a goal before me', she had said, 'I could leap six-bar gates – but how dispiriting tethered on a barren heath'. It was a mistake to be there, she felt, 'where all our doings are without heart and our sufferings without dignity'. The worst element was lack of company as before, only more so. Carlyle had not yet accustomed himself to the circumstance of marriage when being alone as much as he liked was no longer an absolute right. Had he been asked to say frankly how much time per day he felt he should give to seeing his wife, he would have replied half an hour. In the event, the only time she could really have a chat with him was when he was shaving. He often read from 9 a.m. to 10 p.m.; he wrote alone, rode alone, sometimes ate alone, and was inclined to talk as if alone. It wasn't consistently as extreme as this, and they sometimes had wonderful rides together early in the morning, followed by a good breakfast.

Possibly the worst feature was again her health. It was always bad when she hadn't enough companionship to keep her happy, and she now experienced fits of retching and spasmodic writhing that could last from twenty-four to sixty hours! Generally she concealed her condition so well that Carlyle would merely report to his brother, 'Jane is not quite so brisk as she was', or some phrase equally off the mark. One day, she fainted from pain in the head. She could not conceal this from him; but mostly he tended to *over*look rather than look *at* her state with as much attention as he gave to his books. Medical drugs were inefficient in those days, and her doctors prescribed *cold showers* as a remedy. Of course she was not ailing all the time, and frequently picked up; nor can we allow that she was so terribly enslaved to housework drudgery as some have claimed, for she had more help from servants than most women have today; but she was inclined to regard them as extra burdens if not crosses, and may have too often been justified, for at this time one maid seems to have been exposed to constant hysterics, and another served mice with Carlyle's porridge.

They had spent four years at Craigenputtock on the first occasion (1828–31). Would she have to endure another four, she wondered. It was not to be as long as that, and the winter of 1832–3 was spent in Edinburgh, for it was not long before Carlyle began to tire of Craigenputtock and to long for conversation. He did not know himself terribly well. He was *not* a solitary; he was a contemplative, yes, but not a solitary. This ensured that he would never be content anywhere for long. He liked to make a conversational impression, much needing the stimulus of this while his works were still unwritten. But when they got to Edinburgh he found that he was out of practice as a talker. The art seemed to have deserted him. 'I appear like a wild, monstrous Orson amongst the people, and (especially if bilious) smash everything to pieces. The very sound of my voice has got something savage-prophetic'. The result was that he was less popular in Edinburgh than he had been in London. Respect was not withheld from him, but they did not like his manners and were put off by his earnestness. He was put off by their materialism, and was surprised when someone said to him that people 'are quite taken up with making a living'. It had hardly occurred to him that they could be exclusively or chiefly thus engaged, for truly his kingdom was not of this world. He found that in contrast to the 'signs of Birthsong' in London, in Edinburgh 'all is scandalous, decadent, hypocritical, and sounds through your soul like lugubrious universal *Noenia*, chanted by foul midnight hags'.

They returned to Craigenputtock, and once again Jane's spirits fell and she had another bout of ill-health. Once more the silence of the moors was hard to face for any length of time; a silence we can now only experience when a heavy fall of snow stops movement. Thus it was a wonderful break when one day a young American called. Having crossed the Atlantic, a kind of sixth sense compelled him to seek out Carlyle in his northern fastness. It was Emerson. Such a compliment was not lost on them, and they never forgot it. Emerson had nothing to go on except Carlyle's work in the magazines, but he felt that he must visit this man. He was not disappointed. 'He was tall and gaunt', says Emerson, 'with a cliff-like brow, and holding his extraordinary powers of conversation in easy command; clinging to his northern accent with evident relish; full of lively anecdote and with a streaming humour which floated everything he looked upon'. He found him also a good listener, and noted how keenly he appreciated the *democracy* of America where a hardworking boy in a hotel was not just called Boots and left on a starvation level, but was dear old Mongo to be hailed from across the street dining on roast turkey.

✡

13   The Decision

IF Jane was having a very thin time of it at this period, we must remember what Carlyle was contending with. He was in the grip of his daemon – quite literally. He was no free agent. He was certain that he had a great contribution to give to the world. What Carlyle gave was himself, and the world was made richer by his unquenchable aspiration after truth and duty. In the end, Man as Aspirer, raised high above the clods of mud and madness, is what we see symbolized in him. Of course he didn't see it like that. He didn't know that his chief message was his own aspiring soul held up before mankind to inspire mankind. He thought it was to preach this and that, as indeed it was in the first place. At this period he had come to a critical moment in his life. His mind was in a fever of movement. He was consumed with impatience. He was bursting to let out what was in him. He was a volcano not yet in eruption. There floated ever before his mind a Great Idea, and it would not let him rest. He refers to it again and again at this time. We must not think of the Natural on one side, and the Supernatural on the other side, he said. Oh no! 'That the Supernatural differs not from the Natural is a great Truth', he insisted over and over again. The philosophers had grasped this already; 'but they went far wrong however, in this, that instead of raising the natural to the supernatural, they strove to sink the supernatural to the natural'. This was no academic theory on his part, but a feeling: 'A strange feeling of *supernaturalism*, of the fearfulness and wonderfulness of this hurts me and grows upon me... The whole Creation seems more and more Divine to me.' He perpetually lived in this mystic vision of the miraculous that is yet the natural. For him wonder was the basis of worship. 'Is anything more wonderful than another, if you consider it maturely? I have *seen* no men rise from the dead; I have seen some thousands rise from *nothing*. I have not force to fly into the sun, but I *have* force to lift my hand, which is equally strange.' The world was not all dross, as the scientists seemed to be saying, it was all *gold*. Oh, if he could but open all men's eyes to this, would they not cast down their idols and enter the kingdom of heaven even while they were still on earth? He must show that God is not outside but *in* this world, 'and does for ever govern it', and that in the wayward weaving of history we may discern His foot upon the treadle of the loom. What form should he give to his vision? A 'Time-Hat? or a Life of Napoleon? or a history of the French Revolution?'

But now, now he stood at a fearful point in his career! He was thirty-eight. No sense of his life would be made if he did not go forward at once. But the machinery was breaking down, the financial machinery upon which going forward depended. He had left London with commissions for essays in the reviews. But his popularity with the editors was weakening. They were beginning to reject his work now. The general idea was that 'Mr Carlyle is wasting his very considerable gifts.' His personal presence having been withdrawn, he became out of favour, and he was no good at the gentle art of not making enemies. He was extremely arrogant (it calls for some courage to be arrogant when the power is in other hands) and adopted a take-it-or-leave-it attitude, which can scarcely have endeared him to editors. Having written an article on Dr Johnson for Fraser's Magazine he offered it thus: 'I say will *you* of your dog's carrion cart take this article of mine and sell it unchanged? With the carrion cart itself I have and can have no personal concern.' He realized his faults, and in his Journal deplored his vanity. Actually, that vanity was a useful stimulus; but the caged tiger within him, which he could not yet release, made him snarl. Even regarding Mill's new *Radical Review*, he wrote in his Journal, 'Dog's meat bazaar which you enter muffled up, holding your nose, with – "Here, you master, or able editor, or whatever your name is, take this mess of mine and sell it for me – at the old rate you know". This is the relation I am forced to stand in with publishers as the time now runs. May God mend it.' He did nothing to mend it himself by mending his manners. He would not compromise and write in a more popular way : he could not. Things began to get worse when *Sartor Resartus* was at last published in serial form in Fraser's Magazine. No one knew what he was driving at. It seemed the ravings of a literary maniac. The readers of the paper became indignant, and the editor feared ruin.

He had now reached his lowest hour. Would he be baulked? Would he never be heard? Some were saying that he had been led astray, like Edward Irving, who was still descending those stairs – nearly reaching the bottom by now. Carlyle was horrified by his friend's progress in delusion. He had lost his London parish, the more sophisticated of his congregation having forsaken him, and he was now in Scotland preaching on the road. In a letter to the newspapers he declared that 'he did purpose to tarry in those parts certain days, and publish in the towns of the coast the great name of the Lord'. He visited Ecclefechan, from where Carlyle's sister Jean reported how he looked grey, toilworn, and haggard in an immense hat, the country people wild with his rhetoric, but otherwise his name 'an offence in decent society'. That was where popularity had landed him. Carlyle felt a mournful grief for his old friend, together with some degree of humorous contempt and a proper sense of the ludicrous. He called on Waugh and saw where lack of popularity had landed *him*. Waugh had been a mutual friend of Irving at Edinburgh University, a young man of bright prospect and great promise who had gone into literature, writing unsaleable books on Prophecy and Pathology and always expecting a thousand pounds for a good comedy next month. Carlyle found him now in a room in Annandale, 'yellow, wrinkled, forlorn and outcast looking, with beeswax and other tailor or botcher apparatus on a little table, the *shell* of an old coat lying dismembered on the floor', while the one he had on '*demanded* mending since turning was not to be thought of. *There* sate he; into such last corner (with the pale winter sun looking through on him) had *Schicksal und eigne Schuld* hunted the ill-starred Waugh.' When Carlyle came away (with brother Alick), they ordered 4 cwt of potatoes and 8 stone of meal to be sent him (without explanation). 'So goes it in native Annandale', wrote Carlyle to John, 'A hundred times since has that picture of Waugh, botching his old coat at the cottage window, stranded and cast out from the whole occupied earth, risen in my head with manifest meaning.'

Carlyle was as unlike Waugh in his failure as Irving in his success, but he was humble as well as haughty, and while his matchless industry put him in a class by himself, his shrewd nature saved him from incautious expectations. He was often near despair, and longed to be relieved of the burden that he felt had been laid upon him – would that his cup might pass! Yet always the ecstasy on his mountain counted more than the agony in his garden. He would be true to his Vision and listen to his Voice. 'There is none then, not one, that will believe in me!', he wrote in his Journal in the biblical manner he used in order to exhort and console himself. 'Meanwhile continue to believe in *thyself*. Wait thou on the bounties of thy unseen Taskmaster, on the hests of thy inward Daemon . . . and neither fear thou that this thy great message of the Natural *being* the Supernatural will wholly perish unuttered.'

John had been staying with them at Craigenputtock for two months, and was very concerned for his brother when he left. His own affairs were geting brighter, but his brother's darker. Carlyle sought to cheer him up. He foretold a change to come in his outward circumstances as soon as his inward light was clear. He reminded John of the words of Jesus : ' "Be of good cheer, I have *overcome* the world." So said the wisest man, when what was his overcoming? Poverty, despite, forsakenness, and the near prospect of an accursed Cross. "Be of good cheer, I have overcome the world." These words in the streets of Edinburgh last winter brought tears into my eyes.' In the same mood he wrote to Jane, who had gone to Moffat in an endeavour to regain health through water-cure in addition to cold showers. She felt worse. She longed to get back to him. He sought to comfort her. 'Courage, dearest! I swear better days are coming, *shall* come. The accursed, baleful cloud that has hung over my existence *must* (I feel it) dissipate, and let in the sun that shines on all. What is it but a cloud, properly a shadow, a chimaera? Oh Jeannie! ...'

Even as he wrote, the situation was becoming more grave. It began to look as if his pen would not be able to support them. Yet it might still be possible to find a job that would give him a base. It happened that the Chair of Astronomy had fallen vacant at Edinburgh University. Always brilliant as a mathematician (we tend to forget this), he felt qualified. The nomination for this post lay in Jeffrey's hands, and Carlyle made haste to ask his friend once more to help him.

Jeffrey rejected him. This came as a great surprise. Indeed Carlyle was amazed, for when he wrote to Jeffrey it had never occurred to him for a moment that he would let him down. The fact is, Jefffrey had at last lost patience with him. He felt that he had gone astray and was wasting great gifts in mystical musings. He deplored his haughty attitude towards the editors. He was out of sympathy with his excessive earnestness. Above all, he grieved for Jane Carlyle, considering the second sojourn at Craigenputtock a bad thing for her. He thought very highly of Jane, and was in love with her in a sprightly way. He could not bear to see her lose her health and happiness as the caretaker or keeper of a man who largely neglected her. There was reason in all this, if not complete penetration, and he wrote Carlyle a lengthy and unpleasant letter of refusal. Carlyle described it to his brother as 'a polite fish-woman shriek', thus revealing how much it surprised and hurt him. But he took it without show of rancour and replied with careful dignity in his 'choicest manner', which combined courtesy with an assumption of superiority not unmingled with commiseration. He was far from a vindictive man, but he never quite forgave Jeffrey for this, though the latter was soon to acknowledge that he had been wrong about him, for the letter had rashly contained a sentence in reference to himself and Jane which could not be easily overlooked or forgotten. Jeffrey had written, 'Who would not be provoked to see Titania in love with Bottom?'

Nevertheless, Destiny was the main factor in this affair, and was presiding over him. Carlyle knew that somehow all this was for the good, and for the good of his character. 'It is wholesome to have my vanity humbled from time to time. Would it were rooted out of me for ever and a day. My mother said when I showed her the purport of the letter, "He canna hinder thee of God's providence," which is also a glorious truth.' Yes, it was a truth; he could not be hindered or deflected by resistance—though he might have been by too much assistance.

He entered now upon a strange phase. He had been chastened. He had been brought low. At the same time he was lifted up in spirit and expectation, as if the heavens had opened and the clouds of doubt were passing away. 'Neglect, humiliation, all these things *are* good, if I will use them wisely', he wrote. 'From the uttermost deeps of darkness a kind of unsubduable hope rises in me.' The days passed : 'quite original days in my life'. What was happening? He did not know. He was filled with mixed presentiments. He had 'a huge feeling, like one to be delivered from a Bastille; and who says delivered? OR CAST OUT?' He sought for meaning in the passing hours. He paced up and down a high path at Craigenputtock, as on the deck of a ship enstormed and far from shore. He waited. He sat speechless. He listened. It was as if a thousand voices spoke to him 'from the distance out of the dim depths of the old years'. Was not the world all before him, the pains of decision really over, the work ready at hand?—'Oh how fearful, how great!'

Yes, the hour of decision had come at last. He must write a history of the French Revolution. Already in his essays he had been rehearsing some of the vast material—now he must compose it into one mighty work. Second, they must leave Craigenputtock, which was hopeless as a headquarters. If he was to make his presence and influence felt, he must be at the centre of things in London, and make that the base from which to operate. They must go with their capital of £200, and take their chance to sink or swim—if sink, well, they would accept the invitation which Emerson had already extended to them, of going to America. In a spirit of 'judicious desperation' he finally made up his mind that this was the best course, and there was no more hesitation. Jane agreed, but she had sunk so low in spirits that her mood was one of 'diseased indifference'. It was agreed that he would go in advance to London to find a house, while she remained to grapple with the problems of furniture removal. For Carlyle the hardest trial was abandoning his mother. But the great old woman realized the necessity of the movement. She did not seek to restrain him. Even at the last, he said, 'she studied not to sink my heart : she shed no tear at parting'.

14 *Cheyne Row, the Catastrophe*

IT was not long before Carlyle was able to send Jane a detailed account of a house in Cheyne Row, Chelsea. At first she advised caution, but added that in any case 'for me my chief enjoyment I imagine will always be in the society of my own heart's darling, and within my own four walls as heretofore'. He advised acceptance since the rent was only £35 a year, and the situation very pleasant, Cheyne Row being a side street off the Thames which was, in those days, dotted with brown-sailed ships and holiday boats and little steamers that served as part of the city's transport. They took it, and by June 1834 were installed in the house with their furniture, a servant, and Chico, a canary – where they lived as headquarters for the remainder of their lives. Today the house is still there and open to the public (one of the most interesting things of the kind in England), and on a little green island facing the river, not far from Carlyle Pier and Carlyle Mansions, there is a statue of Carlyle himself.

Actually, had he searched London for months he would not have found a more suitable spot. In those days when people walked, Piccadilly Circus was not far away, and in those days when people rode (as Carlyle did a great deal), you could reach the country very soon after crossing the bridge southwards. The three-storeyed house with garden was a good one according to the standards of the day, and an excellent place in which to receive the visitors who came in abundance from all ranks in society. Neither of them ever really appreciated their good fortune in this respect, for unhappily both of them had an infinite capacity for not enjoying themselves, and were always exclaiming to the heavens against featherweight crosses as well as real ones, a wearisome habit in a world 'bursting with sin and sorrow' as Dr Johnson said to Mrs Thrale, who was lamenting too loudly over a lost umbrella.

Nevertheless it is certain that Jane Carlyle from the first clearly saw that she had now achieved a base on which she could stand firmly and face bravely whatever the future might hold. She became determined that they would never leave it. Whenever Carlyle in the years to come was seized by one of his restless moods and a longing to change his abode, she resolutely set her face against it and refused to humour him—much to his benefit. Upon this base she could satisfy the deepest need of her nature, which was friendship. Jane Welsh Carlyle has been celebrated for her cleverness and sharp tongue, but that was only the bright surface of a very emotional, romantic, and warmhearted person. She was frankly adored by a large number of people, women as well as men. Those who came to the house as time went on (often to see her as much as to see her husband) were not only the celebrated, like Dickens, Tennyson, the Tyndalls, the Hunts, the Sterlings, the Froudes, Darwin, Forster, Jeffrey, Ruskin, Mill, Count D'Orsay; but romantic exiles like Mazzini, Pepoli, and Godefroi Cavaignac; *and* unknown people who needed help and sympathy, and who knew that she was as kind and thoughtful as she was brilliant. If they were indiscreet, or phoney, or cadgers (like poor Mrs Hunt), they got short shrift, but Carlyle was surely right when he said that he knew no one who had more sympathy for the wrongs and sufferings of others than his wife.

Edward Irving, never famous for brevity, made a short remark concerning her touch on Cheyne Row which in its artlessness lives in the mind. At this period Irving was back in London, much failing in health. Carlyle tried to see him, but Mrs Irving kept him off. After four attempts, with 'an insuppressible indignation mixed with pity' he forced his way in. He found Irving lying on a sofa. 'He begged pardon for not rising; his wife, who also did not, and, probably, could not well rise, sate at his feet all the time I was there, miserable and haggard.' Carlyle succeeded in raising a laugh in him which set him coughing in a ghostly manner. 'There are moments', Carlyle

wrote to John, 'when I determine on sweeping in upon all
tongue work and choking cobwebberies, and snatching away my
old best friend, to save him from death and the grave'. He could
not save him. Two months later, before setting out for Glasgow,
Irving came on horseback to their door at Cheyne Row. He
looked round the room and, thinking of the woman he had
failed to marry, said to Jane, 'Ah yes, you are like Eve – you
make every place you live in beautiful.' He stayed for a quiet
and sad twenty minutes, then mounted at the door, and was
watched by Carlyle and Jane till he turned the first corner to ride
on away from them for ever.

During this period Carlyle had not yet got started on his
history of the French Revolution. His difficulty was always in
getting a book started, and his mood was very bad at such times.
It is certainly impossible to anticipate the quite devilish mood a
writer may get into if his work isn't going well. Carlyle was an
extreme example of this – vituperative, or silent, or frowning at
the floor while gazing inwardly at unsolved problems. He
couldn't be consoled or helped, for no writer can get others to
assist in solving his problems; he must always be alone in this
respect. Carlyle was also much concerned regarding the financial
situation – for that £200 was running out! That is to say, time
was running out – for to the artist money is time. The position
was 'very grave', he noted with an anxiousness near to desperation. Yet even so he did not propose to yield an inch in
independence of thought, and when the editor of the greatest
daily organ, The Times, offered him a job, he felt impelled to
decline it. When Mr Montagu, hoping to help him with something in the nature of a sinecure, suggested a post in his office at
£200 a year, he repelled the offer as an outrageous liberty. 'The
faith of a Montagu wishing me for his clerk', he wrote to his
brother, 'thinking the polar bear, reduced to a state of dyspeptic
dejection, might safely be trusted to tending rabbits'. He had
hoped to get the editorship of a new review Mill was bringing
out, but it went to a safer man. Carlyle did not conceal his
disappointment at this, but bravely recognized that disappoint-
ments really simplify one's course – 'your possibilities become

diminished; your choice is rendered easier'. His choice was to proceed with a great book on the French Revolution. And now, at the beginning of 1835, he *did* get into it.

Carlyle is our only Historian as Poet, our only Historian as Mystic. All his life he saw things in the light of eternity. Not just when striving to make a literary effect which he knew to be within his power, but always. He lived constantly aware of life's greatest reality, the fact of death. He was continually brooding upon the mystery, as if by sheer intensity of thought he might give, as from a dying man to dying men, an answer and a message. He possessed a great imagination to concentrate upon reality. News of any man's death called out this power in him. 'Man issues from eternity; walks in a Time Element encompassed by eternity, and again in eternity disappears. Fearful and wonderful!' This was no mere truism to him, but a fact with which he daily walked and worked. It gave such grandeur to men. 'Every living man is a visible mystery,' he reflected. 'Say I am a man, and you say all. Whether king or tinker is a mere appendix.' His great heart was ever touched by news of a death. 'Is it not a wild world this? Who made it? Who governs it? Who gets good of it?' Hearing about another, he cried out – 'Oh God, it is a fearful world, this we live in, a film spread over bottomless abysses, into which no eye has pierced' – using those exact words later in *The French Revolution*. Amidst the uproar and the tumult in the pageantry of history, his visionary gaze beheld men as spectres with ends divinely shaped though roughly hewn in the confusion and rumour of the field.

Carlyle was also the Historian as Humorist. Some have considered him the greatest humorist since Aristophanes. This never occurred to him. He knew, of course, that he had a highly developed sense of the ludicrous, but he deplored levity as a deadly sin and earnestly condemned writers who sought to entertain. *Pickwick* was mere 'trash'. Sir Walter Scott had also stooped to please. 'What are his novels, any one of them?' he asked. 'Are we wiser, better, holier, stronger? No. We have been amused.' Yet Carlyle himself could be extremely entertaining, but he hated mirth not based on earnestness and wit not based on wisdom. He knew that a professional comedian was on an almost impossible foundation. Nevertheless, his best historical work is high comedy supported by imagery as powerful as caricature and yet seemingly as exact as a photograph. Herein lay the genius that made it possible for him to make effects that would carry the full weight of his vision, giving it drama and solidity. This part came easily and naturally to him. Looking in for the sake of curiosity at a Radical meeting in London, he noted the strong lung-work of the speakers, and he snapshots the Chairman – 'Cylindrical high head (like a watercan), pot-belly, and voice like the Great Bell at Moscow'. We see the man with marked clarity. We see as clearly his French Revolution figures, whether a Danton or a Robespierre, a Louis or a Camille Desmoulins, a Lafayette or a Mirabeau.

How much high comedy there is even in the low last scene of Marat. He was sitting in his bath on the eve of Bastille Day, 1793. 'What a road he has travelled; – and sits now, about half-past seven of the clock, stewing in slipper – bath; sore afflicted; ill of Revolution Fever – of what other malady this History had rather not name.' In previous pages Carlyle had put Marat's personality before us in harshly humorous lines. He continues now :

'Excessively sick and worn, poor man : with precisely eleven-pence halfpenny of ready money, in paper; with slipper-bath; strong three-footed stool for writing on, the while; and a squalid – Washerwoman, one may call her : that is his civic establishment in Medical-School Street; thither and not else-whither has his road led him. Not to the reign of Brotherhood and Perfect Felicity; yet surely on the way towards that? – Hark, a rap again! A musical woman's voice, refusing to be rejected : it is the Citoyenne who would do France a service. Marat, recognizing from within, cries, Admit her. Charlotte Corday is admitted.'

Carlyle, having at last absorbed the necessary mountain of books on the French Revolution, many of them assembled for him by his close friend John Stuart Mill, had begun work by the autumn of 1834. Once started, he wrote swiftly. He had finished Volume I, which consisted of seven 'books', by the following February. One evening, 6 March, he was sitting with Jane after a long day's work on the first book of the second volume. It was with a considerable sense of relief and satisfaction that he was making such good progress, little anticipating the scarcely believable misfortune which was now about to fall upon him, when John Stuart Mill appeared, looking very white and scared. He seemed so shaky that Carlyle jumped up and took his arm, asking what was the matter. Hardly able to speak, Mill whispered a request to Jane to go down to his woman friend, Mrs Taylor, who was waiting in the carriage below. They both thought that Mill's agitation had something to do with his relations with Mrs Taylor. But that was not it. Carlyle had lent Mill the manuscript of that first volume – his only copy. Mrs Taylor had asked to look at it one evening, and had been left alone to read it at her leisure. There were one hundred and seventy pages of closely written foolscap – for he wrote six hundred words to a page. It would be difficult to mess up a manuscript of that kind so as to make it look like waste paper; but Mrs Taylor achieved this, for next morning a servant lit the fire with it. This was what Mill had come to tell Carlyle. Mrs Taylor soon drove off (not much concerned, we are told) and Jane joined them upstairs. Mill was in such a state of mind that he didn't know what to do, didn't know when to go, and stayed for three hours! Not till he had gone could they fairly face the situation. Carlyle had done his best to take it well, and said to Jane as soon as Mill had left – 'He is terribly cut up by this, we must endeavour to hide from him how very serious this business is to us.' Then they faced the calamity. He had staked all on this venture, it was his 'last throw'. Now it was gone. What was to be done? They spent a dreadful night facing it – Jane comforting him as one would a warrior struck down. By dawn he realized that there was only one course open – somehow, someway, he must *re-write* the volume.

Next day Mill implored him to accept £200. But he would only take £100 – as representing wages for five months' labour.

He was unable to get down to the re-writing at once. He could re-think it, but not re-feel it. 'My work has to be done in a kind of blaze', he once said. And again, a sort of paroxysm of clairvoyance, he declared, was indispensable for getting it done or doing it at all. Assuredly this was not the kind of author whose manuscript one should burn! He was tempted to give up the re-writing, especially as Emerson was again pressing him to move for good and all to America, where he would find many friends and a congenial audience, but Carlyle was not the man to be defeated even by a catastrophe like this. He wailed over small things, but was magnificent over big things. His biographers say that he had thrown away his notes, but I am convinced that this is one of those biographical errors that once too lightly introduced are repeated credulously without sufficient reason. He *could not* have gone forward again without his references and his quotes ready to hand, in a work of this sort. And in July he did start again – and by September, he had finished the volume, which was better than the first, according to Jane.

If this is one of the most hair-raising of misfortunes in the history of literature, the fortitude with which Carlyle met it and the determination with which he overcame it are of the most inspiring examples of bravery and grit ever given by an author.

He then went north to Scotland for a rest. And they needed a holiday from one another. If Carlyle never spared himself, he never spared others either. Jane had been worn down by him as much as he had worn himself down. Now, as increasingly in the years to come, they both made up for tenderness on paper what had been lacking when together, and exchanged most loving letters – for their attraction increased, contrary to Newton's law, in the direct ratio of the square to the distance. 'How I love thee, what think of thee, it is not probable that thou or any mortal will know', he wrote. And she said that if only he would be 'patient and good-natured' with her, she would be ready to do anything on earth for him, but when he 'has neither kind look nor word' for her, then she 'grows desperate and fretful'.

He returned after four weeks, loaded with bacon, hams, butter, and potatoes (Scotsbrig always provided a solid foundation of wholesome food for Cheyne Row—it was sent when he could not fetch it, so there was no question of their ever lacking a full and excellent larder however hard-up they might be). He also brought with him a new servant, Anne Cook, to replace a 'mutinous Irish savage with a face like a polar bear' who had been sent packing. Anne Cook made number five of the remarkable and often fantastic company of assistants who added an abundance of drama, or entertainment, or misery to the Carlyle household.

Now he must get on with the remainder of the work. Authors are subject to many delusions regarding grandeur and success, and with few exceptions are under the illusion that they will have finished their present book long before they do finish it. Carlyle had expected to get done with *The French Revolution* by May 1835. He had done only a third of it by February, and this was burnt in March. On returning from Scotland in December he made a bid to finish it—soon. Having got into it, he uttered, as usual, cries of woe, despair, and agony, and again became so uneasy a companion that Jane, after four months of it, became very ill, and in her turn sought refuge in Scotland. His letters to his 'dear little Janekin' were again most touching, and he seemed almost on the verge of being elated as he made headway into the third volume and began 'to splash down what I know in large masses of colours, that it may look like a smoke-and-flame conflagration in the distance'. When he went away his doting family always saw to it that he got a complete rest. She couldn't get that when she went to her mother, and so, while he really needed some cheerful letters from her when straining at his work, he only got complaints and sarcastic comments on others, and criticisms of her mother – all of which he met with restraint and begged her to come home. She returned, and became quite cheerful again for a time.

When at last he finished *The French Revolution* in January 1837, he felt pessimistic regarding the reception of the book, but said to Jane that he could at any rate say to the world, 'You have not had for a hundred years any book that comes more direct and flamingly from the heart of a living man', reading one of Whitman on *Leaves of Grass*, 'Whoever touches this book touches a man'. Jane did not doubt : 'They can't trample that', she said. To John Sterling he wrote that the writing of it had nearly choked the life out of him, but that it had come hot out of his soul, 'born in blackness, whirlwind, and sorrow', and would somehow be listened to. For in spite of all, as Goethe said

> 'But heard are the voices
> Heard are the sages,
> The world's, and the age's.

15 *The Lectures to London Society*

CARLYLE had now no plans for the future. He assumed that the book would be a commercial failure. He might have to try something else other than literature, or go to America. He felt that 'an infinitude of annoyances and menaces' pressed on him from all sides. He would turn his back on them, however, saying, 'Messrs the Annoyances, do, if you please, make out the result among yourselves'. To John he said, 'My chief pity in general, in these circumstances of mine, is for Jane. She hoped much of me; had great faith in me; and has endured much beside me, not murmuring at it.' Yet it was just at this time that the soundness of his decision to leave Craigenputtock and go to London was made manifest. To a large extent great men create their own circumstances, and may even *be* their own circumstances in an important way. Carlyle's personality and character now affected the circumstances of his life in a most profitable manner: he had so impressed himself amongst influential people in London society that when it was heard that he might accept an invitation to lecture in America, since he appeared unable to support himself in England, they got together – headed by Miss Martineau – and suggested a privately sponsored course of lectures in London. Now, it had always been something of a daydream of Carlyle that he might command an audience and speak directly to a public that way. He had never dreamt that the time would come when two hundred persons, prominent ladies and gentlemen, lovely or learned, lordly or notable, would subscribe one guinea each to hear six lectures from him on any subject he chose to name. Yet that is what came to pass because he was what he was, bound to rise by sheer force of inverse gravitation.

When the idea of the lectures was first put to him, he recoiled, fearing failure. It was a natural reaction, and equally natural, after further reflection and the persuasion of friends, was the return of his old ambition and the hope that he might pull it off – a hope that soon worked into an exciting desire. 'I am to lecture', he wrote to his mother, 'actually and bodily to make an appearance. They are gathering an audience of Marchionesses, Ambassadors, ah me! and what not: all going like a house on fire. The comfort is that I know something of the subject, and have a tongue in my head; one way or another doubtless I shall come through.' He decided to speak on German Literature; to speak, not *read*, since reading a paper never is, and never can be, making a speech, which is, and always should be, giving a *performance*. And he felt that he could give a performance. He chose German Literature because he was full of the subject and had no time for much preparation, as the proofs of *The French Revolution* were already coming in.

That was in March. Again it was natural that as the time drew near for his first lecture in May, he became alarmed and wished that he could run away from the ordeal. But he had really too much grit to funk it, and far more good sense than anxious friends credited him with regarding possible solecisms or failure in tact. He was not a polished man, but, as Froude puts it, 'he was a gentleman in every fibre of him, never to be mistaken for anything else'. In the event, the highly select audience was impressed. His manner and style were not those of a practised speaker, but he was an orator and he held them. His words did not come out smooth and flowing; he often had to grope to find them. He failed to look *at* the audience enough. If at times he distorted his features as if creased by a paroxysm of pain, or broke sometimes into harsh Annandale and gesticulated in an ungraceful manner, there was grandeur in it, and inspiration, and nothing bogus. His own comment was, 'a furious determination on the poor lecturer's part not to break down. I pitied myself, so agitated, terrified, driven desperate and furious; but I found I had no remedy, necessity compelling.' To Emerson he wrote, 'I cannot speak; I can only gasp and writhe and stutter, a spectacle to gods and fashionables'. He described the audience to John Sterling in choice Carlylese, 'My hearers were mixiform dandiacal of both sexes, Dryasdustical (Hallam etc), ingenuous, ingenious, and grew, on the whole, more and more silent'. He had not allowed Jane to come to this first lecture, so she had to await the results. It was with great relief that she could then tell his brother that 'nothing he has ever tried seems to me to have carried such conviction to the public heart that he is a real man of genius, and worth being kept alive at a moderate rate'. Actually the rate was quite good, and he netted £135. Thus, suddenly, the very grave financial situation was overcome – with also a further series of lectures to be booked.

By this time he was thoroughly exhausted. The strain of finishing *The French Revolution* and then grappling with the proofs, while at the same time giving the lectures, had been considerable. Jane urged a complete rest with his family in Scotland, and he set off by sea to be met at Annan Pier by his brother Alick. There is something clear to us even now, eternally vivid to us, in the small fact that he leaned on a milestone (while his brother went off on some temporary business) looking across the Solway and the Cumberland Mountains. He leaned there, tired out. But it was with work *done*, battles fought and finished. He leaned upon his milestone; a solitary dedicated spirit; a visionary; the mountains, the sea, the sky, set before him : the great fact, the great truth we call beauty piercing through his outward to his inward eye in revelation. He remembered that hour all his life. 'What a changed meaning in all that!' he wrote years later. 'Tartarus itself and the pale kingdom of Dis could not have been more preternatural to me. Most stern, gloomy, sad, grand, yet terrible, steeped in woe.'

Scotsbrig was a real haven for him. It was wonderful to have his old home to go to, with his beloved mother there and his brothers and sisters. He may have been wayward and pernickety and spoilt, but none of the family minded, for he never made them feel jealous or sour towards him – they were really fond of him as well as proud. He joined them now for two months, finding the peasant-family household a proper contrast to the London drawing-rooms. He enjoyed complete idleness, roaming

79

at will through places that called up the remembrance of things past but not lost, and visiting the graves of his father and sister. The old brook, Middlebie Burn, still spoke to him by the wayside, still gushed clear as crystal. 'There is no idler, sadder, quieter, more *ghost-like* man in the world even now than I', he wrote to John Sterling – which was his way of saying that he was enjoying himself.

Jane had been ill again at the very time when Carlyle was preparing for the lectures, and Mrs Welsh had been called down to Cheyne Row. Afterwards John had suggested that they all holiday together in Scotland, but they knew it would never work. Now, while Carlyle was happy at Scotsbrig with his mother, Jane was discontented at Cheyne Row with hers. In her present mood she fell foul even of her admirers, the elder Sterlings, who complained that she was too smart with her tongue, and that she would be a more amiable character if she 'were not so damnably clever'. Charles Darwin did not cultivate her acquaintance for he thought she was too self-conscious. Her letters to Carlyle at this time distressed him, for her vivacious line of talk was not a true gaiety. He would have welcomed a touch of melancholy, but feared that even that was lacking. She begged him to return as soon as possible so that they could be unhappy again in the way they had grown accustomed to. When after some delay he did return she wrote a pathetic little note to his mother thanking her for sending him back to her, and saying, 'You have others behind – and I have only him – only him in the whole wide world to love me and take care of me – poor little wretch that I am'.

✡

16 A Dazzling Prospect

WHEN Carlyle returned to London he came in for a surprise. He had purposely stayed away from the centre of things when *The French Revolution* came out, since he expected that it would be ignored or abused or dismissed because of its style. But the qualities of the book won the day, and he found himself prominently before the public. It had been favourably reviewed in the most important quarters by Thackeray, Jeffrey, Southey, Macaulay, Hallam, and Brougham. At first he could scarcely believe in this change of affairs, but as he began to grasp it a great burden fell from him. After joking about how everybody was astonished 'at every other body's being pleased with this wonderful performance', he admitted to 'wild gleamings of a strange joy'. We may be sure that he would have met further rejection with the courage that belonged to him; but it was a great relief not having to do so : 'the late long effort had really all but killed me : not the writing of the book, but the writing of it amid such sickness, poverty, and despair'. He actually felt peaceable. 'Today full of peaceable joy', he noted, now in 1838, at the age of forty-three. Then, thinking that this was going too far for him, he hastened to add – 'ah, no! not peaceable entirely; there is a black look through it still'.

He now followed up the success of the first course of lectures by a second one. In all, he gave four courses, the last being on Heroes in 1840, later expanded and published as the famous *Heroes and Hero-Worship.*

He made heavy weather of it, as usual. When the lecture hour drew near, he would get into a state and appear in the hall looking as white as a handkerchief. But he always did well, and his audience grew larger each time. Whatever he might say to others, he wrote without affectation to his mother. After all, he was the lad from Annandale who hadn't done too badly. 'Among my audience,' he told her, 'I am likely to have some of the cleverest people in this country; and *I* to speak to *them*,' and later as the unexpected scale of success mounted – 'My audience was supposed to be the best for rank, beauty, and intelligence ever collected in London. I had bonnie braw dames, Ladies this, Ladies that, though I dared not look at them for fear they should put me out' – a good, honest touch, that. According to Jane, the quality of the quantity in attendance was unsurpassable, 'there are women so beautiful and intelligent that they look like emanations from the moon; and men whose faces are histories, in which one may read with ever new interest'. One day she had a gleeful surprise; for, as time turned its wheel and preferred its charge, she saw amongst the audience, of all people, Mrs Edward Irving! – the woman who had held Irving to his bargain with such tenacity had now nothing to hold to, and sat there looking plain and thoughtful. '(Jane's 'sympathetic' account of this was a little masterpiece of disingenuousness.)

The financial aspect, for which the whole enterprise had been launched, exceeded their expectations, the figure rising as high as £300 for twelve lectures. Carlyle admitted that this was a great blessing to a man who had lived in 'a bewildering terror of coming to actual want of money'. That this was over now meant very considerable relief. 'It now seems as if I actually might calculate on contriving some way or other to make bread for myself without begging it.' All the same, it was still part of the act to represent himself as almost a pauper. The Chancellor of the Exchequer invited him to a reception. 'Here is the man who disposes annually of the whole revenue of England,' he wrote to his mother, 'and here is another man who has hardly enough cash to buy potatoes and onions for himself. Fortune has for the time made those two tenants of one drawing-room.' He enjoyed exercising his sense of the ludicrous in such representations: 'When grand people and beautiful people pay me grand and beautiful compliments, and I grope in my pocket and find that I have so few pounds sterling there to meet my poor wants with, I can but say with Sandy Corrie – "What's ta use on't?" ' There was a good deal of use on it, and more money was now coming in through the agency of Emerson from America for sales of *The French Revolution*, the instalments totalling some £400. He could now have afforded to take his ease with regard to books, writing without haste as the spirit moved him, while continuing his lecturing once a year as the star turn of the season. It was a dazzling prospect.

He turned away from it.

After delivering one of his lectures on Heroes to an audience that 'sate silent, listening as if it had been gospel,' he confessed to his mother, 'I strive not to *heed* my own notion of the thing, *to keep down the conceit and ambition of me*, for that is it'. He meant this. He was well aware of the temptation to become popular, and was afraid to give way to it. When he came to the end of the course he declared that his performances were 'a mixture of prophecy and playacting', and should be abandoned. He never forgot the fate of Irving blown up by popular wind, and had no delusions about combining popularity with integrity, since obviously he would never be free to say what he really thought about present conditions if he became 'an established popular'. He enjoyed his bit of limelight, but was determined not to be seduced by it – 'whoever he may be that wants to get into the centre of a fuss, it is not I'. There is something touching in his reply to Erskine, a saintly man whom he respected, and who had wished to attend his last lecture. He begged him to keep away. 'I am in no case so sorry for myself as when standing up there bewildered, distracted, nine-tenths of my poor faculty lost in terror and wretchedness, a spectacle to men.' He declared that it was only financial necessity that drove him to it, 'a creature more fit for uttering himself in a flood of inarticulate tears than any other'. A little touching, but also a little ridiculous. He loved uttering himself at great length to a company of six or seven people; now he was being paid to do it to more than seven people who were not allowed to interrupt. Yet the fact remains that he did shrink from the very thing that men who can speak well in public most covet. He never stood on a public platform again until, on a fatal day twenty-six years later, he addressed the students of Edinburgh.

The expanded course of lectures, published as *Heroes and Hero – Worship*, is the most popular of all his works. It certainly

holds perpetual promise of enlightenment, and does create excitement in the reader, and the *sense* of greatness and mystery.
He wrote in such a preaching manner that we tend to forget –
what has been justly claimed for him –that he was one of the
most learned men in Europe; and it is easy to overlook the fact
that while he wrote romantically he did not think romantically,
and would never have seen in Byron, for instance, a true Hero.
'Carlyle, with his vein of peasant inspiration,' wrote Shaw in
one of his passing insights which so often pierced into the heart
of a subject, 'apprehended the sort of greatness that places the
true hero of history so far beyond the mere *preux chevalier,*
whose fanatical personal honour, gallantry, and self-sacrifice, are
founded on a passion for death born of inability to bear the
weight of life that will not grant ideal conditions to the liver.
This one ray of perception became Carlyle's whole stock-in-
trade; and it sufficed to make a literary master of him.' There
are many cases where a brilliant man who has received education, or means to acquire it by his own effort (the only way),
subsequently looks down upon poor parents who have made
this possible for him. Carlyle's father is said to have been grateful that his son did not do this. But there was never the
slightest likelihood of his doing so – he was far too big a man.
Nor did ultimate success turn his head, though it did make him
even more arrogant and overbearing when, accepted as a sage,
he was free to express qustionable, ignorant, or stupid views.
However, it is with special interest that we read the following
on Burns in his essay 'The Hero As Man Of Letters'.

'My last remark is on that notablest phasis of Burns's history –
his visit to Edinburgh. Often it seems to me as if his demeanour there were the highest proof he gave of what a fund of
worth and genuine manhood was in him. If we think of it, few
heavier burdens could be laid on the strength of a man. So
sudden; all common *Lionism*, which ruins innumerable men,
was as nothing to this. It is as if Napoleon had been made a
King of, not gradually, but at once from the Artillery
Lieutenancy in the Regiment La Fère. Burns, still only in his

twenty-seventh year, is no longer even a ploughman; he is flying to the West Indies to escape disgrace and a jail. This month he is a ruined peasant, his wages seven pounds a year, and these gone from him : next month he is in the blaze of rank and beauty, handing down jewelled Duchesses to dinner; the cynosure of all eyes! Adversity is sometimes hard upon a man; but for one man who can stand prosperity, there are a hundred that will stand adversity. I admire much the way in which Burns met all this. Perhaps no man one could point out, was ever so sorely tried, and so little forgot himself. Tranquil, unastonished, not abashed, not inflated, neither awkwardness nor affectation : he feels that *he* there is the man Robert Burns; that the "rank is but the guinea stamp"; that the celebrity is but the candle-light, which will show *what* man, not in the least make him a better or other man! Alas, it may readily, unless he look to it, make him a *worse* man; a wretched inflated wind-bag – inflated till he *burst*, and become a *dead* lion; for whom, as some one has said, there is no resurrection of the body; worse than a living dog! – Burns is admirable here.'

So was Carlyle, on the whole, admirable as he passed slowly from complete obscurity to boundless fame. We may also note, before closing, the fact that apparently he did not wish to avoid quite unnecessary dissonance. Consider : 'My last remark is on that notablest phasis of Burns's history – his visit to Edinburgh'. He could easily have written, 'My last remark is on the most notable phase of Burns's life – his visit to Edinburgh'. No trouble, same statement: but rather than give us anything as clean as that he puts in an 'est' and a 'sis' and a 'hist' and a 'his' and a 'vis' all in a row, plus two extra 't's, three extra 's's and two extra 'i's, not to mention three clashing open 'a's which could have been avoided. The redoubtable Mr John Braine recently dropped the searching observation that a writer's style is the sum of his reading life. Yes indeed, the best way to learn how to write is by reading the masters. From Carlyle one can learn *nothing*. Yet he was a great writer. He makes his impact. It is a man speaking directly to us; none other like him – we do not need him polished. He does not always get across by any means, but that was the only way he knew how. His contemporary, William Cobbett, always got across. Yet Cobbett's scheme of commas, was, strictly, fantastic, even ludicrous. His italics even more so. (Cobbett's *Autobiography* was published in the 'Thirties, without the italics! – an incredible effrontery.) But the slightest alteration would have been an injury : for there he is, in person, standing over us, speaking to us, with us, at us – as only he could. Carlyle has no scheme of commas, nor of anything else really : the wonder is that he succeeded as often as he did.

[*Radio Times Hulton Picture Library*]

Carlyle 1846. By Lynch after a daguerrotype

Thomas Carlyle

[*Radio Times Hulton Picture Library*]

Thomas　Carlyle

[Radio Times Hulton Picture Library]

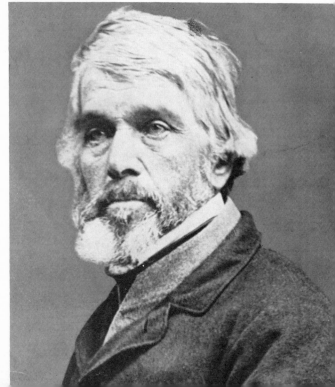

✿

17   Carlyle and his Contemporaries

THESE lectures and *The French Revolution* brought him into touch with more people. The celebrities and the fashionables of the day solicited his friendship and enjoyed his company. A man of great parts in those days was Monckton Milnes who knew how to gather good talkers together who would make 'striking remarks' – not hoarded for publication (as today) but willingly produced and passed round. Carlyle used to say that if Christ were again on earth Milnes would ask him to breakfast, and at the Clubs everyone would be talking about 'the good things' that Christ had said. There was strong mutual regard between Milnes and Carlyle. This led to more friendships, especially with Edward Baring, who became Lord Ashburton, and whose wife, the Lady Harriet, was to share with him a close attachment to Carlyle.

Thus his circle widened. Carlyle liked *gentlemen* – as they then were. He liked their cultivated manners lacking in conde-scension, their brand of humour, the felicitous way they avoided friction. He accepted invitations to country week-ends, though always careful to complain afterwards at the resultant state of his nerves and digestion, and he certainly found it difficult to cope with the elaborate idleness and with the too-zealous assistance of flunkeys. His eye took in everything and remembered every-thing : few writers have equalled, and not even Dickens sur-passed, the swift likeness :

'Lady Holland is a brown-skinned, silent, sad, concentrated, proud old dame. Her face, when you see it in profile, has something of the falcon character, if a falcon's bill were straight; and you see much of the white of her eye. Notable words she spake none and sate like one wont to be obeyed and entertained. Old Holland, whose legs are said to be almost turned to *stone*, pleased me much. A very large, bald head, small, grey, invincible, composed-looking eyes, the immense tuft of an eyebrow which all the Foxes have, stiff upper lip, roomy mouth and chin, short, angry, yet modest nose.'

The number of swift portraits which Carlyle made – and we could never mistake the signature – include sketches of Peele, Queen Victoria, Lamb, Count D'Orsay, Mill, Tennyson, Dickens, Gladstone, Wordsworth, Macaulay, Hunt, Emerson, and some others as well known or less known. There is no malice or jealousy; the attitude is generally that of lofty commiseration, the mode that of harsh humour. If it were not for the humour (often in terms of physiological exactitude or caricature) his superior airs would offend more frequently. He thought nothing of poetry. He had once tried to write in verse, and failed, but did not realize that condescension towards poets was unbecoming on his part. He elected to overlook the fact that Tennyson was a poet and praised the man, but all lovers of Keats feel that Carlyle stained his own name by the *faux pas* he made. Milnes had written a book on Keats, and Carlyle described it as 'an attempt to make us eat dead dog by exquisite currying and cooking', and declared that 'the kind of man that Keats was gets ever more horrible to me. Force of hunger for pleasure of every kind, and want of all other force.' Malice would have been preferable to that tone and that ignorance of the subject. Having read a volume by Wordsworth, he said that all he could remember was a picture of a wren's nest, and alluded to the poet as 'a genuine but small diluted man'. He was so defective in literary judgement that he was unable to discern that Wordsworth could pack into eight classic lines of deathless verse ('A slumber did my spirit seal . . .') everything that can be felt about death, in comparison with which his own long set pieces on the subject are as delicate as the gait of a hippopotamus. Indeed, it is with a feeling akin to indignation that one reads such a remark made about the only English poet who had the guts to travel over to Paris to find out about the French

Revolution and nearly perish in it – and that that remark was made by a man who said to his wife in April 1848 that he could not report on a 'revolution' in the streets of London because it had begun to rain and he had come out without his umbrella.

Having failed to write a novel himself, he was equally condescending about Dickens, without a notion of how the genius of the novelist towered over his own achievements, while his strictures on poor Lamb have boomeranged to a degree that would have surprised him, for he did not understand the tendency of the English to shrink from a hard view of a soft man. 'Insuperable proclivity to *gin*, in poor old Lamb,' he wrote. 'His talk contemptibly small, indicating wondrous ignorance and shallowness, even when it was serious and good-mannered, which it seldom was; usually *ill*-mannered (to a degree), screwed into frosty artificialities, ghastly make-believe of wit; – in fact more like "diluted" insanity (as I defined it) than anything of real jocosity, "humour", or geniality. He was the *leanest* of mankind, tiny black breeches buttoned to the knee-cap and farther, surmounting spindle-legs also in black, face and head fineish, black, bony, lean, and of a Jew type rather; in the eyes a kind of *smoky* brightness or confused sharpness; spoke with a stutter; in walking tottered and shuffled.'

Yet Carlyle was by no means always ungenerous. He hailed Ruskin (twenty-four years younger) with real pleasure and was delighted to find a man saying things in the political field more forcibly and effectively than he could himself. He made many complimentary remarks about Ruskin and even attempted to soothe the poor old father who was appalled at his son's views in *Unto This Last*. In his turn, Ruskin looked up to Carlyle as his master, declaring him to be 'born in the clouds and struck by the lightning'.

But in the end it was Ruskin who was the more critical – of Carlyle the man. There came a time – for one moment only I take the liberty of going forward as far as the 'Eighties, after Carlyle's death – when Ruskin confessed to the anger he had felt at Carlyle's habit of moaning, 'never seeming to feel the extreme ill manners of this perpetual whine', while at the same time putting forth the strength necessary to the production of his *oeuvre*. Ill manners is exactly what it was, but no one had ever dared to point this out to him; he never realized it himself, beyond once admitting that 'the Universe is not wholly made for me, but for cocks also,' and that 'we are very despicable drivellers to make any moan'. But he remained practicaly unaware of this main fault until it was too late. Ruskin went on to say, 'What in my own personal way I chiefly regret and wonder at in him is, the perception in all nature of nothing between the stars and his stomach – his going, for instance, into North Wales for two months, and noting absolutely no Cambrian thing or event, but only increase of Carlylian bile'.

At one point in the relationship between these two men, when Ruskin was forty-eight and Carlyle was seventy-two, there occurred a curious incident when Ruskin's behaviour was distinctly unfortunate. Ruskin, who had begun to declare that the writer he felt to be nearest his heart was the bitter satirist and pessimist, Swift, was passing through one of his periods of depression, when he became subject to hallucination and fits of madness. At such times he was inclined to see his fellow men as a lot of Yahoos who must needs hate the highest when they see it. One day Carlyle was amazed to discover, on turning over the pages of a political treatise by Ruskin, called *Time and Tide*, that he, Carlyle, had alleged that in the streets of Chelsea he could no longer walk abroad without receiving insults, simply because he was a grey old man and cleanly dressed – two conditions which qualified him for brutal treatment by the revolting mob. These assertions of the disciple were too much for the master, and as they were quite untrue he publicly protested on behalf of a vast multitude of harmless neighbours' who behaved both towards him and towards each other 'in an obliging, peaceable, and perfectly human manner', and he insisted that the views attributed to him by Ruskin were 'altogether erroneous, misfounded, superfluous, and even absurd'. These denials of the master were too much for the disciple. No longer concerned with facts, Ruskin expressed himself as deeply pained at 'the most insulting terms' being applied 'to the man who probably of all men living most honoured you'.

Ruskin never whined and always kept clear from any parade of personal solemnity or portentousness, but he had been so spoilt by easy circumstances and too-early triumphs that he did not know how to deal with any kind of opposition when it came – it amazed him, whether it came as opposition from the female sex or as an attack upon his political writings. Happily, a reconciliation was effected between him and Carlyle after some further correspondence. We can understand Carlyle being annoyed by Ruskin's representation of his relations with his neighbours, for he knew himself to be well-liked in Chelsea, just as he knew (as others could not) how many anonymous people loved him for the help he gave them, in various different ways, in the most unassuming manner. He was so well-known by the generality of those who used the bus service in Chelsea that one day when a stranger observed to the bus conductor that 'the old fellow 'as a queer 'at,' the conductor answered – 'Queer 'at! Aye, he may 'ave a queer 'at, but what would you give for the 'ed-piece what's inside of it?'

One day Froude had just left Carlyle's door and was going down the Row when he was approached by a bright, eager girl in her late 'teens who asked him if Thomas Carlyle lived there. He showed her the house, and 'her large eyes glowed as if she was looking upon a saint's shrine'. Easy for us to smile and say – how little she knew! But the incident does underline an important thing about Carlyle – he made a noble impact upon his generation. There is always solid substance behind myth. The fact is, Carlyle endeared himself to a large number of people. He was revered, and the esteem was cast abroad. We have only his written works, and many a harsh description of contemporaries; we do not have the tone of his voice, we do not see his eyes which were 'of a deep violet, with fire burning at the bottom of them, which flashed out at the least excitement'. It is worth noting that John Tyndall, one of the finest scientists and also one of the very best writers of the nineteenth century, revered Carlyle, truly loved him, and regarded his task of looking after him when at last he travelled north to receive the Rectorship of the University of Edinburgh, as the greatest privilege of his life.

He was to see 'the stern grandeur' on the dead face of Jane Carlyle, and in his essay on Carlyle he draws attention to the words with which Froude described the dead man's face, in which there was no sternness – 'He lay calm and still, an expression of exquisite tenderness subduing his rugged features into feminine beauty. I have seen something like it in Catholic pictures of dead saints, but never, before or since, on any human countenance.' And there is something instantly affecting in the simple sentence with which Tyndall closed his account: 'So passed away one of the glories of the world'.

There was something about Carlyle. He seems to have been off-hand in his appreciation of Dickens, but according to Froude, Dickens 'loved him with all his heart'. The rent was raised in Cheyne Row for other inhabitants, but not for Carlyle. In those days the U.S.A. pirated the work of British authors, but Carlyle was paid.

He was even liked by individual Irishmen who met him. This seems to me conclusive that there was something about him, for he was fond of representing Irishmen, during the most terrible period in their history, as a lot of senseless braggarts and aimless layabouts, degraded, corrupt, and mendacious; and their spokesmen as the 'chief quacks of the then world'. He had no understanding of what the English were pleased to call 'the Irish Question', while his views on the future of Ireland were as audacious in their frivolity as his remarks upon 'Nigger emancipation' and his reference to the 'Indian mutinous hyaenas'. Determined to regard Cromwell as a moral hero, he seems to have been equally determined to make out the Irish as an impossible people, chiefly composed of 'lying slaves'. One day, in 1843, when in East Lothian, he saw 'some hundred and fifty decent Highlanders', and nearby a concourse of wild Irishmen, 'aimless, restless, hungry, senseless, more like apes than men; swarming about, leaping into bean-fields, turnip-fields, and out again, asking you "the toime, Sir" '. He wondered why 'the country did not rise on them and fling the whole lot into the Firth'. Perhaps he was right about them; anyway it is a fair sample of his manner of talking about Irishmen, and those men might well have been pardoned if they had thought it a good idea to throw *him* into the river as a fair comment on his comments touching the Irish Question. However, when he paid a visit to Ireland, when he passed through Bray in County Wicklow, saw the Dargle in Powerscourt's Domain, looked upon the lonely white road that leads to Glendalough, and felt the lure in the distances and the sadness in the evenings, he seems to have been humanized by the scene and to have reflected with justice upon the engines of tyranny. He was received with great affection by Gavan Duffy and John Mitchell. A small thing perhaps, but worth mentioning, and pondering upon.

✖

18 Restlessness

FOLLOWING the Lectures in the 'Forties and his expanding social life, it might seem that he could now have shared with Jane a happier and easier life after a quarter of a century of struggle. But again he was full of lamentations over the hardness of his lot! To us it seems shameful. Here was a man whose dreams of fame and recognition had come true. He had worked hard and won. He had made a great decision and it had been proved right. His ship had come home. Many literary men's ships do not come home; they sink and are abandoned; or, not sinking, never reach land, their captains yet determined to ride out the storms or go down, content if far from shore, at least to be 'far from the trembling throng, Whose sails were never to the tempest given'.* Carlyle had been more fortunate. Yet he still groaned. He talked of the 'insupportable burden and imprisonment', of the 'abominable pressure', of the 'immeasurable, soul-confusing uproar' of London life. He could have good company but not solitude at the same time – how unfair. 'Welfare,' he declared, 'at least absence of *ill* fare and semi-delirium, is possible for me in solitude only'. He added, wryly, 'Oh, the devil burn it!' – quoting the exclamation of the Irish corporal when flogging a soldier who seemed dissatisfied with the affair, 'there is no pleasing of you, strike where one will'.

He could laugh at himself, he could not reform himself. When he was passing through one of his almost insane, and certainly abnormal, moods, he was an uneasy companion in the home, and an imperfect citizen in society (which he was anxious to reform). Asked to attend a jury he was so overcome by 'the stew of lies, and dust, and foul breath', that he sought exemption after two days. But in the following year (1841) he was called to

* Shelley's *Adonais*

another jury, could not get out of it, and made himself the while nearly impossible for Jane to cope with. To almost any author such a summons would have been considered as a useful experience and perhaps a good bit of copy. When it came to the point, Carlyle, who regarded it as a monstrous infringement on his time, nevertheless not only turned it into comedy, but proved himself to be the only effective member on the jury. He uttered cries of pain when writing his books, but not when writing his letters, which were sometimes better. And on this occasion our humorist had full play. The trial was about Patent India-rubber Cotton-cards (whatever they were). Who was the inventor of same? Already £10,000 had gone into this case because of there being 150 witnesses. By the end of the second day all the jury had to do was to give an obvious verdict. But they couldn't, for one obstinate man held out against the others, and had already starved out three juries. Carlyle discerned at once that there was nothing in his head – 'which resembled a Swedish turnip' – save obstinacy. 'It was a head all cheeks, jaw, and no brow, of shape somewhat like a great ball of putty dropped from a height.' Asking the others to leave the man to him, Carlyle got him in a corner and set to work on him. He congratulated him on being a 'man of decision', a man capable of having an opinion of his own 'in these weak days', and able to stand by it, a quality most rare and precious. But was he being fair on this occasion? Should he use his strong mind to take undue advantage over the weak minds of others, and cause perhaps another £10,000 to be run up? Was it right of him, was it really just? Very soon he had won the man over, and they were all free to go home.

Thus Carlyle displayed ability and easy mastery in a situation where others were at a loss what to do. He was not an unpractical dreamer. There was no good lending library in those days for serious readers and scholars. He it was who, in 1840, gathered powerful men around him and founded the London Library which has ever since been a life-line not only for general readers but for searchers in every department of knowledge. It was a practical achievement of the highest merit and of permanent benefit.

His restlessness at this time was excessive even for him, he was like a kind of wild horse – to get *out*, to gallop away somewhere was what he blindly sought. In his Journal he entered, 'My wife, herself seemingly sinking into weaker and weaker health, points out to me always that I cannot go; that I am tied here, seemingly as if tortured to death'. If she did her best to tie him down, she was well advised, for here was a man who married or unmarried; successful in his endeavours or foiled; in the city or in the wilds, would cry out in sorrow for himself.

Shortly after the Jury sitting they rashly went north *together* and took a cottage by the sea in a place called Newby, in the Annandale district. On the way, they stayed the night in her mother's house at Templand. It was necessary for them to share the same bed. And a cock crowed. Two disasters for Carlyle. He tossed and turned, unable to sleep, then suddenly in the middle of the night got up, rushed out of the house, took a horse and rode over to his sister at Dumfries, from where he dispatched an anguished note to Jane: '. . . Would to Heaven I could hear that my poor Jeannie had got some sleep! I have done little but think tragically enough about my poor lassie all day: about her, and all the history we have had together. Alas! let us not take the tragic side of it . . .' We do not know what Jane had to say about this, nor what Mrs Welsh said, we can guess what they thought. There followed a particularly dispiriting 'holiday'. Carlyle knew all the places around intimately since boyhood, but he visited no one, spoke to no one (sadly realizing that he gave offence thereby), preferring to hold converse only with 'the Titanic elements, spirits of the waters, earth, wind, and mud', regarding the whole venture afterwards as one of 'confused pain, partly degrading, disgraceful', costing about £70. Jane's tribute was characteristically forthright: 'Oh such a place! Now that I am fairly done with it I look back upon it all as a bad dream! never shall I forget its blood-red, moaning sea – its cracked looking-glasses, its industrious fleas, its desolation and hugger-mugger such as hath not entered into the heart of man to conceive.'

19 Death of Mrs Welsh

IN 1842 Mrs Welsh suddenly became ill, and before Jane Carlyle had got more than half-way to Scotland she died.

Jane had not got on well with her mother, and they had had such unfortunate rows when together in the same house that Carlyle had been obliged to intervene with conciliatory advice to his wife to bear with her mother's humours. There was little to excuse the daughter's behaviour on one evening – the only one in fact – when a party of notables was to be held at Cheyne Row. Mrs Welsh lighted a show of candles so much in excess of what Jane conceived suited to the household economy that she removed two of them. Her mother was very hurt and shed tears. Later on Jane so deeply regretted her action that she left instruction in her Will that two candles were to be preserved and to be lit upon her coffin when she died.

In spite of the rows, they had doted on each other, had needed each other, and their exchange of loving words had never been the mere defensive endearments of a dutiful relationship. 'Oh, my dear friend, what a shock for you! And what a loss! The loss of one's mother!' Jane wrote to her friend J. G. Cooke, sixteen years later, on the death of his mother. 'Yes, the longer one lives in this hard world motherless, the more a mother's loss makes itself felt, and understood, the more tenderly and self-reproachfully one thinks back over the time when one had her, and thought so little of it.' And she added that since her own mother died, 'Not a day, not an hour has passed since that I have not missed her, have not felt the world colder and blanker for want of her'.

She had reached Liverpool where she was to stay overnight with her uncle and family, when the fatal news came. She collapsed, and could go no further. She was quite cast down, realizing so suddenly what she had lost, and she was thrown into exaggerated self-reproach for the things she had left undone for her mother, and the words she had left unuttered. If Carlyle had been self-centred when asked to attend a jury, he was almost faultless now. He grasped the situation at once, told her to stay where she was, and laying aside his work went to Scotland himself to carry out the legal business involved with Mrs Welsh's estate. There was a good deal of negotiating to be gone through (regarding the Craigenputtock property, etc) with factors, sub-factors, a certain Duke's farm agent, and so on. This took two months, and amazingly, Carlyle didn't seem to mind much (he was close to his family at Scotsbrig), and did not become unduly restive until, realizing that the agents were being incredibly slow in their resolutions for no better reason than that it would be inconsistent with the Duke's dignity to go fast, he began to express himself in suitable Carlylean terms about 'the accursed, soul-oppressing puddle of Dukery', and to declare that all the Dukes in creation melted into one Duke were not worth sixpence to him.

Meanwhile, hearing regularly from his wife in letters utterly despondent and hopeless, he did his best to console her in the quite useless preachy way that came too easily to him. But there was more than facility in one remark which he dropped on the way, when he observed that 'all the faults and infirmities of the departed seem now what they really were, mere *virtues imprisoned*, obstructed in the strange, sensitive, tremulous element they were sent to live in' – a consideration worth thinking out by any of us ever capable of applying it *pre mortem*.

While he was making an inventory of Mrs Welsh's furniture at Templand, he wondered whether instead of the misery of a sale, it might not go to Craigenputtock which could be used in future as a county *pied à terre*; but Jane firmly opposed the plan, fearing, no doubt justly, that he might then abandon Cheyne Row in one of his wild moods, and this she was determined to avoid, since London was the only place where she could be unhappy in reasonable comfort. As soon as she had put her foot down, Carlyle gave in, saying – 'I cannot deliberately mean anything that is harmful to you'.

They returned to Cheyne Row in the summer of 1842. Jane

was so low and sad that Carlyle suggested that she should accept an invitation from Mrs Buller (the mother of his former pupils), who admired and loved her, to go to their family place at Troston in Suffolk. She went, and as the attentions of kind friends always had a good effect on her, she cheered up a little. It was a quiet life there, conducted with such ethical propriety that on Sunday when out for a drive in the evening, Mr Buller always *walked* the horse on principle, and Jane could not evade the Church services officiated at by Reginald, the youngest son, now parson at Troston. Her spirits rose at the opportunity offered for satirical comment at the expense of Reginald, whose manner of delivery left room for improvement. She represented him as 'pausing just when he needed breath, at the end of a sentence or in the middle of a word, as it happened! In the midst of this extraordinary exhortation an infant screamed out – "Away Mammy! Let's away!" and another bigger child went off in whooping cough! For my part, I was all the while in a state between laughing and crying; nay, doing both alternately.'

20 Past and Present

WHENEVER Carlyle had decided upon a great historical subject suitable to his genius and his mission, he then declared it to be *impossible*. He had now resolved to do a work on Cromwell – and cried out again and again, 'Oliver is an *impossibility*'. All was mud and misery, dust and darkness. He could not shift the stones. He would never raise the building. He covered himself with reproaches for sinful and disgraceful sloth. Yet he hung on, he always did, in spite of dejection and despair, still peering through the mist for meaning – and always found it in the end. But his high standard and his close scrutiny of what invariably seemed intractable material discouraged his hope of success, and he could never believe that he would do what he did do in the end.

However, just at this time, the beginning of 1843, he had a literary break. He turned aside from the big historical work and wrote *Past and Present* without difficulty in six weeks! He was appalled at the social misery of the age, worse for the poor than it had ever been, and nearer to revolution – 'eleven thousand souls in Paisley alone living on three-halfpence a day, and the governors of the land all busy shooting partridges and passing Corn-laws the while'. *Past and Present* gave a clear picture of English life in the twelfth century, contrasted that picture with the 'free men' of the modern era, and asked who were the real slaves and serfs? It was one of those powerful and passionate works which change public attitudes and promote progressive laws. Without such opinion-makers as *Past and Present* and *Unto This Last* harsh and absurd theories of political economy cannot be undermined, nor factory acts introduced. Such books are deeds.

Before Carlyle had completed his last course of lectures, he had preceded *Past and Present* with his short book called *Chartism*. One could not learn from it what Chartism actually was, and very few parts of it can now be read with the stimulation that Ruskin could give to similar themes, for never has there existed a writer less capable of succinctness than Carlyle. We yearn for him to come to the point. His long sentences can be tedious, and he never discovered the short sentence. We easily lose the thread, get lost, and either start a paragraph again or give up. Yet his powerful spirit triumphed, and he carried the day in his day and smashed the policy of *laissez-faire*. His radical-conservative, anti-revolutionary views – much akin to those of William Cobbett – were highly original and effective in his period. And when in *Chartism* he comes out with his particular brand of sorrowful humour he still carries us with him.

'New Poor-Law! *Laissez faire, laissez passer!* The master of horses, when the summer labour is done, has to feed his horses through the winter. If he said to his horses: "Quadrupeds, I have no longer work for you; but work exists abundantly over the world: are you ignorant (or must I read you Political Economy Lectures) that the Steamengine always in the long-run creates additional work? Railways are forming in one quarter of this earth, canals in another, much cartage is wanted; somewhere in Europe, Asia, Africa or America, doubt it not, ye will find cartage: go and seek cartage, and good go with you!" They, with protrusive lower lip, snort dubious; signifying that Europe, Asia, Africa and America lie somewhat out of their beat; that what cartage may be wanted there is not too well known to them. *They* can find no cartage. They gallop distracted along highways, all fenced in to the right and to the left: finally, under pains of hunger, they take to leaping fences; eating foreign property, and – we know the rest. Ah, it is not a joyful mirth, it is sadder than tears, the laugh Humanity is forced to, at *Laissez-faire* applied to poor peasants, in a world like our Europe of the year 1839!'

Past and Present did its work but cannot make as great an impact on the present day reader. Nevertheless, we can still see through the window he opened on to mediaeval England with some fascination. His chief source was a chronicle written by Jocelin of Brakelond, an old St Edmundsbury monk, written in Monk-Latin. 'The language of it,' says Carlyle, 'is not foreign only but dead : Monk-Latin lies across not the British Channel, but the nine-fold Stygian Marshes, Stream of Lethe, and one knows not where! Roman Latin itself, still alive for us in the Elysian Fields of Memory, is domestic in comparison. And then the ideas, life-furniture, whole workings and ways of this worthy Jocelin; covered deeper than Pompeii with the lava-ashes and inarticulate wreck of seven hundred years!' But Carlyle loved nothing better than to lever up from the dusk and darkness of great libraries chunks of fact and set to work on them and give them life. He loved groaning too at the pedantry he encountered : 'Alas, what mountains of dead ashes, wreck and burnt bones, does assiduous Pedantry dig up from the Past Time, and name it History; till, as we say, the human soul sinks wearied and bewildered; till the Past Time seems all one infinite incredible grey void, without sun, stars, hearth-fires, or candlelight; dim offensive dust-whirlwinds filling universal Nature; and over your Historical Library, it is as if all the Titans had written for themselves : DRY RUBBISH SHOT HERE!' Apparently he thought that the people who supplied him with the raw material for his art should themselves have been artists! Was this modesty or arrogant conceit? – it was certainly inartistic on his part to have mentioned the Dry-as-dusters at all.

Anyway he himself did possess the gift of imagination, the power to see what is there, and the art to make us see it. 'This England of the Year 1200 was no chimerical vacuity or dream-land, but a green solid place, that grew corn and several other things. The Sun shone on it; the vicissitude of seasons and human fortunes. Cloth was woven and worn; ditches were dug, farrow-fields ploughed, and houses built.' He is enough of a magician to make it all real and present for us. True, it is never possible to enjoy the whole of any of Carlyle's books. Over and

over again we have to wade waist-deep, even neck-deep in
words, till we feel like drowning, and wonder if we will reach
one of his glorious landing-places of solid fact – and no artist
ever took greater care to accumulate telling detail. Of course
when his prophetico-exhortationary mood is combined with the
incorrigible humorist, it is good fun. 'Consider, for example, that
great Hat seven-feet high, which now perambulates London
Streets,' he writes in Book III, *Past and Present* :

'The Hatter in the Strand of London, instead of making better
felt-hats than another, mounts a huge lath-and-plaster Hat
seven-feet high, upon wheels; sends a man to drive it through
the streets; hoping to be saved *thereby*. He has not attempted
to *make* better hats, as he was appointed by the Universe to
do, and as with this ingenuity of his he could very probably
have done; but his whole industry is turned to *persuade* us
that he has made such! He too knows that the Quack has
become God. Laugh not at him, O reader; or do not laugh
only. He has ceased to be comic; he is fast becoming tragic.
To me this all-deafening blast of Puffery, of poor Falsehood
grown necessitous, of poor Heart-Atheism fallen now into
Enchanted Workhouses, sounds too surely like a Doom's-blast!
I have to say to myself in old dialect : "God's blessing is not
written on all this; His curse is written on all this!" Unless
perhaps the Universe *be* a chimera; some totally deranged
eightday clock, dead as brass; which the Maker, if there ever
was any Maker, has long ceased to meddle with? – To my
friend Sauerteig this poor seven-feet Hat-manufacturer, as
the topstone of English Puffery, was very notable.'

To us, such an advertisement must seem very far from a
topstone! The nineteenth century prophets got no more than a
whiff of mechanization and quackery, but they sniffed it keenly
and reacted strongly, and fearfully – without a notion of what
was yet to come in terms of audacious mendacity and of the
insane extremities in the cause of amenity. Think of Ruskin's
reaction to railways – or Wordsworth's! Jane Carlyle, in a letter

to her husband in 1845, dropped the remark, 'All these prodigious efforts for facilitating locomotion seem to me a highly
questionable investment of human faculty; people need rather to
be taught to sit still.' In 1826, Willam Cobbett, in his *Rural
Rides*, tells how he asked a woman the way to a certain village
about four miles away – but she did not know.

'Pray, were you born in this house? – Yes. – And how far
have you ever been from this house? – Oh, I have been *up
in the parish* and over to *Chute*. That is to say, the utmost
extent of her voyages had been about two and a half miles!
Let no one laugh at her, and, above all others, let not me,
who am convinced that the *facilities* which now exist of
moving human bodies from place to place are amongst the
curses of the country, the destroyers of industry, of morals,
and, of course, of happiness. It is a great error to suppose that
people are rendered stupid by remaining always in the same
place. This was a very acute woman, and as well behaved
as need be.'

Today, we have been so battered by 'progress' of every kind
that we are almost too numbed to cry out, or even to feel strongly
any more. When Lockhart read *Past and Present*, he said that it
had made him *conscious of life and feeling* as he had never been
before. That is the main thing about Carlyle : he could raise his
readers up and make them feel. His power to do this lay in
certain passionate beliefs which were really feelings. 'He was one
of those who heard the Veritable Voices of the Universe', wrote
G. K. Chesterton. 'Nature's Laws,' declared Carlyle in a typical
passage, 'are eternal : her small still voice, speaking from the
inmost heart of us, shall not, under terrible penalties, be dis-
regarded'. After expanding this theme he goes on, ' "Rhetoric" all
this? No, my brother, very singular to say, it is Fact all this.
Cocker's Arithmetic is not truer. Forgotten in these days, it is as
old as the foundations of the Universe, and will endure till the
Universe cease . . . unless indeed the Law of Gravitation chance
to cease, and men find that they *can* walk on vacancy.' He

believed that truth prevailed over falsity and right over wrong. It is easy to see that in the long run truth must prevail over what is false, since truth is the fact, truth is what is, while a lie is based upon what is not – and so cannot compete for long (a notable short-term example being Nazi propaganda during the last war). But such a reasoning, calculated belief does not affect us much, it has to be *felt* before it can be a force in us. Carlyle did feel that he had special news of this kind, and it gave him extra power which affects the reader.

But as a thinker he was even more unsatisfactory than most prophets. He shifted his views about so much and so unclearly, and came to talk so emphatically about the Strong Man, that many people thought he meant that Might was Right instead of Right prevailing in its ultimately mighty way. Many of his political views were so absurd that to even mention them at this date is unnecessary. People were puzzled still more when he brought out *Latter-Day Pamphlets* in 1850 in which he ironically attacked the philanthropists and intellectual radicals and other supporters of the oppressed, in very much the same way as Tolstoy attacked the Russian radicals and progressives – though both writers were passionate champions of the poor.

Carlyle often gave the impression that he was too aloof. A man called Glassier, who knew Ruskin, Carlyle, and William Morris, said, 'With Ruskin the people are You; with Carlyle they are even further off, they are *they*; but with Morris the people are *we*'. Nevertheless, when Carlyle's great heart was really stirred and his imagination fired he was perhaps a more effective voice for the inarticulate than anyone else. There the men stood, he says in *Past and Present*, at the time of the 'Manchester insurrection', silent in the streets, putting 'their huge inarticulate question, *What do you mean to do with us?* in a manner audible to every reflective soul in the kingdom'.

21   *Aspects of Life with Carlyle*

CARLYLE was now faced with Cromwell again, and so was his wife, as he did not keep his groans to himself but shared them with her. He meant no harm, he never did, but he was unable to restrain his irritability. He would wildly complain about noise, or food, or servants, or the state of his health, all unaware, till after Jane's death, that he was slowly undermining *her* health – for she concealed this from him. It was not difficult to conceal it, for he noticed nothing. He was not so much lost in thought as in thoughtlessness. Having paid her attentions during courtship he gave her rather little attention during marriage. She wilted under Cromwell, who became as much her enemy as sulphur became the enemy of Frida Strindberg, and she told a friend that the sight of the old folios and illegible manuscripts pertaining to the Protector were enough to give her lockjaw. However, now in 1843, seeing that he was getting exhausted again, and that he had expressed the desire to visit certain battlefields concerning his subject, she suggested that he take a holiday, and he set out for Wales.

Carlyle and his wife lived at Cheyne Row from 1834 to 1866. But they did not live together all that time. They separated for some years. Not during a consecutive period but at frequent intervals – in fact some thirty times. He went almost yearly to Scotland, twice to Ireland, once to France, once to Belgium, twice to Germany, as well as many times to Surrey, Devon, and Wales on visits to friends; while she frequently went north to her kindred in Liverpool and Scotland – and sometimes, while one was on the way out, the other was on the way in. Whenever they attempted to holiday together it was disastrous. Even travelling together to a given point didn't work : once when they were both in the north and about to return she wrote to him saying that she would prefer to travel back alone as 'I might need to have a window shut when you preferred it open' – a sentence which speaks volumes. These holidays from one another, when added together, make in sum a good many years. They both hated travelling and made heavy weather of the simplest journey, complaining at the smallest discomfort, but it was essential as an aid to matrimonial peace. The pity is that there was nothing planned or organized regarding these breaks, and Carlyle was so utterly indecisive about any day of departure that the exasperated Jane found it futile to pack a bag for him till the last minute.

Apart from the undeclared reason that it was a good thing for them to have these separations, there was the fact that if Carlyle didn't down tools at intervals he would have been worn out and good for nothing. There was also a third reason sometimes – namely, Jane's desire to have him out of the house while repairs were carried out in Number 5 Cheyne Row. She had a passion for house-renovation – no less. Again and again she filled Number 5 with carpenters, painters, plumbers and other workmen, tearing up the place and even falling through the ceiling, till the house was like Bedlam or the sack of Troy, as she described it. She enjoyed this. It brought into play her organizing ability and her desire to superintend chaotic scenes. So long as she had Carlyle out of the house she was content, and if he threatened to return too soon she warned him off. Sometimes she even admitted that she liked these occasions : 'To see something going on, and to help its going on, fulfils a great want of my nature.' Yet also she could carry it out in the spirit of Mrs Gargery with a touch of Mrs Gummidge. Indeed, at one point, Carlyle taxed her with this and called for less Mrs Gummidgery, though a more inappropriate person than himself to lodge such a plea can scarcely be imagined, since his own Gummidgery was excessive, for again and again he would refer to himself as the lonest and lornest of creatures on the whole of the then occupied earth.

Having thus parted in July 1843, they were free to become very affectionate again, and in a few days he was writing, 'Oh

Goody, I send thee a hundred kisses. I have much need to be
kissed by a Goody. Adieu, adieu.' She was glad to have him out
of the way, and got on with turning the house upside down with
the aid of a painter, two carpenters, a paper-hanger, two
apprentices, and a foreman, all hurrying and scurrying about
'affording the liveliest image of a sacked city!' The smell of
paint was so strong that she had to leave her windows wide
open; but since the men left ladders behind overnight she was
afraid of thieves, and was obliged to go to bed armed with a
dagger, a pistol, and a police-rattle. During daytime she sought
refuge from the smell by putting up a tent in the garden
constructed with the aid of clothes-lines, under the shade of
which she retreated with 'writing materials, sewing materials,
and a mind superior to fate'. All this was quite exhilarating, and
there was the pleasure of writing it up in the manner in which
she excelled. 'The only drawback to this retreat,' she told her
uncle, John Welsh of Liverpool, 'is its being exposed to "the
envy of surrounding nations"; so many heads peer out on me
from all windows of the Row, eager to penetrate my meaning!
If I had a speaking trumpet I would address them once for all –
Ladies and Gentlemen, I am not here to enter my individual
protest against the progress of civilization! nor to mock you with
an Arcadian felicity which you have neither the taste nor the
ingenuity to make your own! but simply . . .'

Needless to say, the practical work carried out by the workmen and by herself was thorough. The walls were painted or
papered, the floors washed, the beds taken to pieces and remade,
the furniture mended. She herself had re-covered chairs and
sofas, and stitched carpets and curtains. Always with an eye to
her husband's comfort and requirements, she had arranged a
library that contained every essential for the peaceful working-
room he had specified before leaving. She knew him too well to
expect that he would notice much of her improvements, but she
always studied his comfort as if he had been the most observant
of men – which he only fully realized when she was dead. He
did sometimes think of her while she was alive – if on holiday. I
mean, he brought his mind to discern her nearly as keenly as

upon an historical person. He had ended his tour of about three months by visiting the Dunbar battlefield, and had also gone to Haddington. From there he had written, 'These two days the image of my dear little Jeannie has hovered incessantly about me, waking and sleeping, in a sad but almost celestial manner, like the spirit, I might say, of a beautiful dream. These were the streets and places where she ran about, a merry, eager little fairy of a child . . . My dearest, while I live, one soul to trust in shall not be wanting.'

In the last letter which Jane had written to her mother she had said sadly, 'How one is vexed with little things in this life! The great evils one triumphs over bravely, but the little eat one's heart away.' It is a curious fact that this obvious truth should be so evaded. If only 'petty' things were really petty it would be all right, but they are the sum of life, they make two-thirds of our day. To be able to confront the annoyances with restraint should be regarded as the ultimate in courage, and the person really outstanding in this as a hero. But not only do we fail to do this, we allow the conventional heroes to claim exemption from this most important aspect of bravery. Carlyle was a prime example in preferring such claims. Returning home after three months, he was reasonably satisfied with the improvements for a few days, but then – a neighbour played a piano! This being opposite the room which Jane had prepared so carefully for him he declared that he couldn't work in it, and all the workmen had to be called back again to make further alterations, with the result that his bile increased tenfold because of the tumult and the shambles he himself had caused. Jane could write amusing accounts of this sort of thing in letters to her friends, and to that extent she achieved the artist's power to overcome the world by turning vexation into comedy, but she was careful to add – 'Alas, one can make fun of all this on paper; but in practice it is anything but fun'.

Jane had now to suffer under the composition of *Cromwell* as a rehearsal for what she was later to suffer under the composition of *Frederick the Great*. Not getting into his subject at first, he fell into a sulphurous mood and became such an uneasy companion that Jane often felt like leaving him for good. Her health deteriorated so much that she was obliged to go to her relations in Liverpool for two months in 1844, and again in the following year, while he stayed where he was, except for short visits to his society friends, the Barings, in Surrey. In thanking a friend for the present of a book, she said she had found it waiting for her 'after an absence of two months in search of – what shall I say?' She wasn't sure why she was 'visited with these nervous illnesses which send me from time to time out into space to get myself rehabilitated'. She did not like to admit, even to herself, that the cause was her husband. And once she was away, the old affectionate terms were resumed, and she wrote to him from Liverpool saying, 'It is curious how much more uncomfortable I feel without you, when it is I who am going away from you, and not, as it used to be, you going away from me'. Then, recalling their recent rows over Cromwell, she added, 'I am always wondering since I came here how I can, even in my angriest mood, talk about leaving you for good and all; for to be sure if I were to leave you today on that principle, I should need absolutely to go back tomorrow to see how you were taking it'. Whenever she had time to reflect, she was capable of counting her blessings. She was fond of her uncle and cousins; but when she saw at close quarters the kind of life they lived, she felt sorry for them. When she contemplated the essential emptiness of her cousins' life, the dressing three times a day, the total lack of seriousness about anything, the girls' longing for a bit of excitement, she felt compelled to say – 'How grateful I ought to be to you, dear, for having rescued me out of the young-lady sphere!' And certainly that is exactly what he had done.

Nevertheless, she enjoyed being with them and other friends, in the midst of whom she shone. She expressed the hope that, so long as he was neither too miserable nor too content on his own, she would stay away as long as possible for she liked to have her 'human speech duly appreciated'. That was it. She liked to be the centre of attention and was not content with her 'character of Lion's wife'. She was anxious to preserve her 'I-ity', as she had charmingly put it to John Sterling, though there was never any danger of her losing it. One morning she came down to breakfast and found that everyone else had finished. On inquiring why the bell in her room had not rung, she was told that as she had been so witty the night before, it was thought best to let her sleep on as long as possible in case she felt exhausted.

There was an additional advantage regarding conversation unattended by Carlyle. It could be less constrained and more fun. Now that he had achieved fame and was written about as 'the first man in Europe' everyone thought it proper to be very earnest and solemn in his presence, to watch their tongues, to come out if possible with wise remarks or searching observations, and generally put the best foot forward. She told him that 'one of the penalties of being "the wisest man and profoundest spirit of the age" is the royal one of never hearing the plain, unornamented truth spoken', and that therefore people who only bored him were much more interesting with her. She was greatly loved by a large number of people of all kinds and both sexes – of this there can be no question. We might suppose that so clever a woman could have been more feared or respected than loved. A glance at that pert, forthright, no-nonsense face, as portrayed in the 1838 Samuel Lawrence sketch, suggests that it would be risky to take a liberty with her. And indeed her whiplash tongue could be sharp enough. Among the hangers-on at Cheyne Row was a certain bishop. One day he had the temerity to complain of her coldness to him, and wrote her a foolish letter. She did not reply. Soon afterwards he called, and she told him outright that she had not answered his letter because it seemed to her 'the best way to counteract the indiscretion of his having written it'. (A model rebuff? Yes indeed – but if a man were to say this to a woman he would be thought a cad.) Once, entering a baker's shop she heard the baker say to a bewildered little man with a wooden leg, 'I'll tell you what to do. Go and join some Methodist's chapel for six months; make yourself agreeable to them, and you'll soon have friends that will help you in your object'. The little man looked doubtful and unhappy at this. 'Nothing like religion for gaining a man friends,' added the baker, and then rashly turning to Jane Welsh Carlyle, inquired,

'Don't you think so, Ma'am?' She fixed her dark eyes full on him and said – 'I think that whatever this man's object may be, he is not likely to be benefited in the long run by constituting himself a hypocrite'. Such a reply sprang from a full, rich nature, not a coldly moral one. She had a certain star-like quality, said Geraldine Jewsbury. She sparkled. But there was fire in that flint. There was no limit to the depth of her passionate affections. Thus she was surrounded by adoring friends, some brilliant, celebrated, and powerful; others humble, exiled, unbalanced, broken or bereaved. 'I never knew a heart more open to the sufferings of others,' said Carlyle.

✿

22   *The Fascination of Jane Welsh Carlyle*

CARLYLE was delighted with Jane's letters from Liverpool, though he praised them with a touch of foolish condescension. It is a sad fact that she never had the slightest public recognition of her literary talents during her life, and the high-minded people who abused Froude after Carlyle's death deplored the opportunity he provided for her posthumous fame.

Lytton Strachey suggested in his essay on Carlyle that she 'might have become a consummate writer or the ruler and inspirer of some fortunate social group'. It is easy to see what she would have become in our age. There is almost no true 'literature' now; nearly all the art of words goes into journalism, much of it good, and flows over into radio and television where the journalists foregather again in various panels. Jane Welsh would have been an independent person shining on paper and verbally – probably not completing any long sustained book. She was essentially a journalist of genius. All dullness and triviality she edited from her *jour*, and used the rest as the material for her art, 'working up the squalid difficulties into a work of art', as she herself put it. She could portray character and summon up a whole scene and life-atmosphere in a few words, either through direct description or reported conversation. 'He reminds me,' she said of a certain Dr Weber, 'of a statue that had been perfectly polished in front, and left rough-hewn behind, to stand with back to the wall'. She kept in touch all her life with her marvellous old Haddington nurse, Betty ('I never saw such perfection of attachment, and doubt if it exists elsewhere', Carlyle was to write). She saw her when visiting her old aunts who lived at Craigenvilla and were so pious that they fell into a panic if they forgot to say grace before a meal. In a letter from there, Jane wrote, 'I was regretting to Betty that my aunts should live in such a fuss of religion. "My dear," said she, "they were idle – plenty to live on, and nocht to do for't; they might have ta'en to waur; so we maun just thole them, and no compleen." ' Her combination of comedy and character-drawing and social history, all done in a few words, is worth more than a passing glance. It is not surprising that Dickens, judging from what he saw of her correspondence, thought her the best woman writer of the day – (though it is strange that he did not get her to write for *Household Words*). Indeed, her report on a visit to Pentonville in a letter to her uncle, John Welsh, strongly reminds one of Dickens himself :

'We went to hear their religious teaching in the chapel. An under-chaplain stood on the altar with a Bible in one hand and a red book (like a butcher's) in the other; he read a passage from the Bible, then looked in the red book for the numbers (they have no names), whose turn it was to be examined. For instance, he read about the young man who came to Jesus, and asked what he should do to be saved? Then after consulting the red book he called out, "Numbers thirty-two and seventy-eight : What shall I do to enter into eternal life?" Thirty-two and seventy-eight answered, the one in a growl, the other in a squeal, "Sell all that thou hast and give to the poor". ... Now, my blessed uncle, did you ever hear such nonsense? If a grain of logic was in the heads of thirty-two and seventy-eight, mustn't they have thought, Well, what the devil are we taken up, and imprisoned, and called criminals for, but just because we take this injunction seriously, and help you to carry it out, by relieving you of your watches and other sundries. I should tell you too that each prisoner has a bell in his cell! One man said to some visitor, "and if I ring my bell a fool answers it". '

The three volumes (it is said there could have been almost twice the amount) of *Letters and Memorials*, edited by Carlyle and Froude, make a portrait of a woman which has not been surpassed. Sparkling and forbidding women, like Nancy Astor or Margot Asquith, are not common, but are far from unique, and in exerting and exhibiting themselves are not dissimilar. Jane Welsh resembled no one else. She disliked clever public women and feared what she felt to be their coldness, being particularly put out by Lady Ashburton's use of the phrase 'all about feelings' to disparage display of emotion. Since great warmth was central to her nature, her astringent remarks are the more enjoyable and telling, as when she writes, 'people who are so dreadfully devoted to their wives are so apt, from mere habit, to get devoted to other people's wives as well!' or, 'Women, they say, will always give a varnish of duty to their inclinations. I wonder whether men are any better in always giving to their disinclinations a varnish of justice'.

One of her correspondents to whom she wrote most freely was John Sterling (who thought her the best letter-writer in the world). There was a celebrated book of the day by Tieck called *Vittoria Accoramboni*, and Sterling had sent it to her, thinking that the heroine would be a woman after her own heart. For an understanding of Jane Carlyle it is important to know her reply:

'. . . But you said nothing of the man after my own heart, so that Bracciano took me by surprise, and has nearly turned my head! My very *beau-idéal* of manhood is that Paul Giordano; could I hear the like of him existing anywhere in these degenerate times, I would, even at this late stage of the business – send him – my picture! and an offer of my heart and hand for the next world, since they are already disposed of in this. Ah! what a man that must be, who can strangle his young, beautiful wife with his own hands, and, bating one moment of conventional horror, inspire not the slightest feeling of aversion or distrust! When a man strangles his wife nowadays he does it brutally, in drink, or in passion, or in revenge; to transact such a work coolly, nobly, on the loftiest principles, to strangle with dignity because the woman "was unworthy of him", that indeed is a triumph of character which places this Giordano above all the heroes of ancient and modern times; which makes me almost weep that I was not born two centuries earlier, that I might have been – his mistress – not his wife!'

Sterling was taken aback. And that was the point, of course. She was always quite without humbug, without cant, while Sterling, and Carlyle, were not without their brand of solemn, masculine cant which did not appeal to her. She was in her forties when she wrote that letter, and it amused her to lend the book, with her marginal marks in it, to high-minded men friends who were then duly shocked.

Since the *Letters* do give a fairly full portrait of a person, they therefore do not always show her in a completely favourable light. When she made a literary judgement in passing, we are not always impressed, as when she expressed 'no feeling but remorse for wasting mortal time on such arrant nonsense' – in reading *David Copperfield*. One can even be irritated by her too conscious avoidance of cliché in her letters, to avoid even an accepted idiom by turning it round and writing 'heels over head' instead of 'head over heels'; or 'still-stand' instead of 'stand-still'; or 'butter and bread' instead of 'bread and butter'; or 'undershoots the mark' instead of 'overshoots the mark'.

Sometimes one is surprised by the arrogance of a strangely narrow view. For example, she had no use for Bishop Colenso. His story is good nineteenth-century stuff, and highly diverting, though not as well known as it ought to be. As a missionary in Zululand he had attempted to expound the Bible to the supposedly 'backward niggers', but had met with the most intelligent questions and arguments which he could not answer – particularly with respect to the recorded passage through the Red Sea by the Israelites in a single night. Paying attention to the statistics in the Bible concerning this operation, the savages took the liberty of pointing out to the bishop that even if the Israelites had advanced in close order *five abreast* – irrespective of baggage, sheep, and cattle – they would have formed a column one hundred miles long. Therefore they could not have passed across the Red Sea in a week, let alone in a night. Colenso, recognizing the good sense of this, and assuming that the Church would be glad to welcome a corrective of biblical statistics in the cause of accuracy, brought out a book embodying the necessary emendations, called *The Pentateuch Examined*. But the book raised a storm of abuse, excessive even for theologians. The bishop was unfrocked, and the number of volumes then published to 'expose' his heresy amounted to one hundred and forty (yes, 140 which can be counted in the catalogue of the British Museum Reading Room). It is needless to add that today those volumes are seen to be worthless while the Zulus and Colenso are seen to be sound. Jane Carlyle knew about the affair, but in a letter to a cousin her only comment was, 'Have you heard of the wonderful Bishop Colenso? Such a talk about him too. And he isn't worth talking about for five minutes, except for the absurdity of a man making arithmetical onslaughts on the Pentateuch, with a bishop's little black apron on!'

Probably she was ill-informed concerning the complete controversy, and wrote simply out of distaste for theology in general and bishops in particular, for she never could abide those little black aprons. Once she remarked to Mrs Russell, who had sent her a book on evolution, 'If there is one thing I dislike more than theology it is geology'. And she went on to comment, 'When Darwin in a book that all the scientific world is in an ecstasy over, proved the other day that we are all come from shell-fish, it didn't move me to the slightest curiosity whether we are or not. I did not feel that the slightest light would be thrown on my practical life for me, by having it ever so logically made out that my first ancestor, millions of millions of ages back, had been, or even had not been, an oyster.' Fair enough, from that angle of course – especially as it is put with such wit and candour. The Scientist says how things have arrived. The Thinker appraises the philosophical significance to be deduced from that means of arrival. The Poet is lost in wonder that they have arrived at all. The Woman, *per se*, prefers to keep her eye on the problem of survival.

No doubt Carlyle influenced her attitude towards Darwinism, for he was fond of making satiric remarks on the subject; he certainly must have influenced her in cultivating the habit of complaining after having enjoyed herself. For instance, in one of

her most irresistibly lively letters (to Carlyle in 1845) she described attending a play and meeting Tennyson, Dickens, Forster,
Count D'Orsay, Nell Gwyn, and the famous actor, Macready
(who was a friend of Carlyle, recognizing in him something of a
fellow play-actor). Jane had a great time, all of them making
much of her and kissing her. But she ends up with, 'Between
eleven and twelve all was over – and the practical result?
Eight-and-sixpence for a fly, and a headache for twenty-four
hours! I went to bed as wearied as a little woman could be. . .' She
could not see how silly it was to add those words, just as Carlyle
could not see how silly and ill-mannered it was to go to the
Ashburtons at the Grange, meeting there, according to his
Journal, 'Lords Lansdowne and Grey; Thackeray, Macaulay,
Twisleton, Clough, a huge company coming and going'. Yet
carefully adding, 'Lonely I, solitary almost as the dead. Infinitely
glad to get home again to a *slighter* measure of dyspepsia, inertia,
and other heaviness, ineptitude, and gloom.' No doubt G. K.
Chesterton was right in saying that 'disease ran athwart his body
and his mind' and that, while praising silence, he had to talk and
talk and write and write to prevent himself from going mad.

In following the life-story of Jane Welsh Carlyle – and perhaps
changing our opinion of her each time we meet her, as we often do
with people we know around us – the question sometimes ob-
trudes, Who would have made her happy as a married woman?
Thirty years after her wedding-day she wrote, 'I married for
ambition, Carlyle has exceeded all that my wildest hopes ever
imagined of him, and I am miserable'. Exactly: she married for
ambition, and the price was heavy. Had she married George
Rennie she would have been thoroughly disgruntled in about ten
years because of his lack of genius. Had she married Irving the
result would soon have been appalling. Earlier I suggested that
she might have done well with a cultivated and successful statesman – but would she have stood that kind of social racket? I think
she had a greater capacity for friendship than for wife-ship. There
is no question but that she was greatly loved by many people.
When Thackeray was ill, it was to her he turned. When the elder
Sterling was dying, it was to her he turned. Real tests.

Jane Carlyle (1801-
1866)

[*Radio Times Hulton
Picture Library*]

James Anthony Froude (1810-1894). Carlyle's friend and biographer
[*Radio Times Hulton Picture Library*]

Her best friend was Geraldine Jewsbury. ('My most intimate friend in all the world', she wrote nine years before her death.) This friendship was the most searching test of all. Geraldine, some twelve years junior to Jane, was a very emotional person, continually falling in love with both men and women and swearing everlasting friendship. In spite of this she never married, and was free to develop a considerable literary talent, and in the end became widely respected as an advanced minor novelist. Though over-emotional, she possessed a fund of north country common sense, practicality, shrewdness, and perseverance – qualities she inherited from her father, who was a Manchester industrialist. Having fallen under the spell of Carlyle's books, Geraldine Jewsbury fell under the spell of both of them in person. To the end she regarded Carlyle as 'a preternatural being', the nobler of the two, but remained always passionately attached to Jane. Carlyle came to respect her a good deal in the end, though he never approved of her coming out so strong on Love, and deplored her partiality for the works of George Sand, which he detested to about the same degree as Tolstoy did, though for reasons opposite to those of the over-sexed Russian. Geraldine never ceased to venerate Carlyle, but her comments on him as an ordinary mortal were valuable. For instance, Carlyle has been represented as being vastly entertained in the evenings by his wife's masterly descriptions of incidents of the day, people she had met, etc; and eventually he substantiated this in his memoirs. I am sure it was true some of the time, and especially near the end, but the norm is likely to have been nearer to Geraldine's idea of it, which somehow rings true : 'He took no earthly interest in what she had seen and done and asked questions in an absent indifferent way that would have made me mad – but she told him quite pleasantly. Do husbands *ever* make themselves pleasant companions? But *why* should they not always?'

The frustrating conditions imposed on women in the nineteenth century, narrowing the outlet for their affections, often tended to make women's friendships peculiarly poignant and strong. Geraldine Jewsbury and Jane Carlyle became very close, though at first the relationship was rather one-sided, Geraldine being the more attached and more often in need of advice from her friend who was too ready to be sardonic. But Jane's advice was worth having. Geraldine was frequently on the brink of marrying or wondering how to get out of a marrying situation. There is something delicious in the forthright, ruthless, feminine flashing sense in Jane's reply to a question, – 'Only fools marry for the sake of keeping a promise'.

For some years Geraldine was in the weaker position, and made exceptionally jealous scenes when she felt neglected; but at length the roles were reversed and it was Jane who, regarding Geraldine as her special acquisition, became jealous, not in a fury of brief tantrums, but in door-shutting sulks, when *she* felt neglected. In fact, shortly after Geraldine had left the north and come to live in Chelsea, and Jane had written that glad letter to Mrs Russell saying what a wonderful thing it was that her 'most intimate friend in all the world' would be living as close to her as Oakley Street, she broke with her! She complained that Geraldine was paying too much attention to others. She refused to see her, ignored her advances, showed her friends extreme rudeness on every opportunity, and made it appear that the estrangement could not be healed. But her qualities and Geraldine's loyalty were such, that the latter would not allow the tie to be broken, especially as she claimed to know eight years in advance that Jane was 'fading from the category of human beings, and entering into the mysterious family of those who are – dying'. The breach was healed, and Geraldine ministered to her in every way until the end. And it is Geraldine Jewsbury who, writing to a friend called Mantell, made the most generous and perhaps the most notable of all the *dicta* regarding that bright and melancholy soul: 'She is one of those who cannot be judged but must be accepted. She is a *heroine* and right or wrong makes a prescription for herself. If she is cruel sometimes and hard, at others she is more noble and generous than ninety-nine just persons who need no repentance, and as to her *fascination* I appeal to yourself!'*

* See Susanne Howe, *Geraldine Jewsbury*

✴

23   The Battle against Noise

IF Carlyle was glad to get Jane's letters from Liverpool, she, as always, looked forward to and depended upon his admitting that it made a very palpable difference to her temper throughout the day if she got a letter to begin with. Apart from his theme-song, 'Courage! courage! better times *will come*', he wrote almost gaily. She had left a pet leech in his care and he assured her it was 'leading a very quiet life of it, never even asking what is taxes'. He laughed at himself for pitying squires' daughters riding in the Park, and to his 'dearest Goody' he signed himself, 'Ever your affectionate, *bad* T.C.'. Since the death of her mother he had always taken care to remember her birthday, and his present to her now (6 July) touched her, 'Oh my darling, I want to give you an emphatic kiss rather than to write . . .' But when she was about to return to Cheyne Row, he set out again for Scotland. He spent a day with her in Liverpool, and then went by boat amongst its 'distressing and disgusting uproars' for Annan. She went south to London.

Shortly after returning she was engaged at one of her main tasks in looking after Carlyle – that of protecting him from noise. Indeed the constantly recurring battle against noises occupies a leading theme in the high comedy of Carlyle's life. He could *not* work or sleep or think if any untoward sound could be heard. It hardly mattered where he was – the country was no better than the town. In fact, at this very time at Scotsbrig he was complaining of the combination of noises he had to bear in the early morning: 'cocks, pigs, calves, dogs, clogs of women's feet, creaking of door-hinges, masons breaking whinstone, and carts loading stones'. In short, life was taking the liberty of going on. Carlyle was never actually a mad man, but at intervals noise could drive him mad. One recalls Ruskin's remark to a pious person who had talked of 'the Lord' having a hand in the fact that he had gone off his head : 'Your note to Joan is extraordinarily pious for *you*! and not a bit true! It is not the Lord's hand, but my own folly, that brings these illnesses on me; and as long as they go off again, you needn't be so mighty grave about them. How many wiser folk than I go mad for good and all, or bad and all, like poor Turner at the last, Blake always, Scott in his pride, Irving in his faith, and Carlyle because of the poultry next door!'

Yes indeed – the poultry. In those days people often kept hens in London, and this caused calamities at Number 5 Cheyne Row. One day, looking down into the yard of Number 6, Jane was horrified to see some hencoops. This would be the end! She dared not tell Carlyle, he would know soon enough when the cock crowed at dawn. Her bedroom was directly below his, and she got no sleep anticipating what would happen if it did crow – and it did. He leapt from his bed in a delirium of anguish and rage, and thumped about his room. No more rest for anyone that night, nor subsequent ones. What was to be done? Should they poison the hens? Or shoot them? – this was coolly considered, Jane claiming that it would look best in court if she did the shooting. But she managed otherwise; she always did manage one way or another. She *wrote them down*. Her letter to the neighbours was so seductive as to be irresistible, and they gave up poultry. She had to undertake more than one anti-hen campaign, sometimes employing more devious means, but was always successful. Carlyle was grateful to her; but it was not till after her death, when she had become as real to him at last as his historical characters, that he saw her as his saviour, his protector, his heroine – 'Oh, my Heroine! Endless were her feats in regard to all this, and her gentle talent too. I could not have lived here but for that, had there been nothing more.' And now, on returning from Liverpool, it was a dog, a terrible dog, disturbing the peace at all hours. Could she cope with this crisis before he came back? A very serious question, for this dog promised to be worse than the hens. However, she succeeded in writing it down also.

✖

24 *Darkening of the Scene: Lady Ashburton*

BY now a certain *modus vivendi* had been established between them which assured a renovation of affection from time to time when necessary. But circumstances were arising which began to chill Jane's heart, to sour her mind, warp her character, and still further undermine her constitution.

Fame had brought Carlyle in touch with a great many people. Some just wanted to visit him, others wrote seeking advice from the sage – Should I become an author, and if so how? What must I do to be saved? I have such an ugly face that my life is a misery, what advice can you give me? He nearly always replied with care and courtesy and patience, for in the wings he was the most compassionate of men, hardly ever refusing anybody anything, least of all money, which he gave freely to any poor soul who asked for help. On stage he was not terribly democratic. He saw no particular merit in town workmen or peasants *per se*. Unlike Strindberg who was ashamed of being the son of a servant, or Tolstoy who felt guilty at being the son of a landowner, he was without complex regarding class. Though immensely proud of his peasant parents, he never felt called upon to approve the company of average countrymen, referring once to the 'babbling inconclusive palaver of the rustic population here if you have anything to do with them'. Harmless fellow passengers – cattle dealers and the like – in the sleeping rooms of a ship, comprised 'a brutal element of human savagery'. Servitors found him unsympathetic. 'A 'dirty scrub of a waiter' at the Bell Inn, Gloucester, had complained of his tip, which Carlyle reckoned liberal. 'I added sixpence to it, which produced a bow which I was near rewarding with a kick.' He was never in favour of meeting impertinence with meekness, or ignoring it. In a railway carriage, a man in company with a pampered young lady in a tiger-skin mantle ventured to smile openly at his hat. Carlyle looked him straight in the eye with a regard which signified – 'Miserable ninth part of a fraction of a tailor, art thou sure that thou hast a right to laugh at me?' The woman turned pale and the smile died on the face of her companion. 'When a man is just out of a section of Bedlam, and has still a long confused journey in a second class train, that is the time for getting himself treated with the respect due to genius.' He could poke fun at himself in this vein, but he never lost the uncommon touch.

What he liked was the upper-class English gentleman with his attitude of *noblesse oblige*. He thought that attitude more widespread than it actually was. When, at a dinner party, Lord Ashburton (as Edward Baring had become) was handed a note, Carlyle much admired the way he instantly got up without the smallest fuss or explanation, left the room, and swiftly putting on riding-boots, galloped away into the stormy night – for he had been informed that a labourer's house was on fire. It was indeed entirely typical, and still is, of that kind of man, but unfortunately not typical enough to save England from a failure in aristocracy equal to its failure elsewhere. Carlyle's increasing reputation – especially after the publication of *Cromwell* which he had finished by 1845 – made him very welcome in these circles, and it was at the town and country houses of the Ashburtons that he was most often seen, a guest more favoured and courted than almost any other. Here he fell under the spell of Lady Ashburton.

Everyone did. Probably her photographs do her an injustice, for they reveal a lady too largely built to be beautiful rather than handsome, and so elaborately draped that it is impossible to visualize her figure though we may guess her carriage. She held undisputed place as one of the chief society women of the period. The fact that as an aid to this she was in possession of three or four residences with a retinue of servants, a shooting-box in Scotland and a special railway carriage to command, would not necessarily have given her more of a reputation than that of a 'well known society hostess', but she was a superior character, an imperial personage, a real *grande dame*, without affectation or humbug, unimpressed by the pretensions of privilege or the ostentation of wealth, delighting in cultivated and informed conversation. She discerned the superiority of Carlyle and revelled in his talk, the sheer entertaining quality of which we know little, just as from his books we cannot hear his great laugh which so often accompanied and corrected his verbal excesses. She had a depth of feeling which she concealed under a contempt for sentimentality, and so well understood the importance of not being too earnest in public that she often presented a mien of mockery. Carlyle had never known anyone like her; she was imperious to him, issuing orders, even interrupting his discourse to speak to a parrot – this was a novelty and he found it irresistible. He became romantically attached to her. He saw her as 'the beautifulest creature in all this world, divided from me by great gulfs for evermore'. She became 'his Queen', she was as 'the lamp of his dark path', she was 'his Beneficent', and he was 'the dark man that shall again see the daughter of the Sun'.

Previously Jane had never worried about Carlyle in relation to other women. He was not tempted by his female adorers. He had nothing of the flirt in him, nothing of the philanderer: he could never be drawn into the luxury of the brief encounter. But as his friendship with the Ashburtons ripened, she began to become anxious – and annoyed. It had never occurred to her that another woman of equal brilliance with herself would engage his interest, and that that woman would be the foremost society hostess of the day. Carlyle, who felt no sense of guilt about this – because sexual intimacy did not come into it – was merely concerned that his wife and Lady Ashburton should get on well, and indeed an effort was made by both ladies to like each other. At first Jane succumbed to her charm as did all others, male or female. But it did not last. When she and Carlyle went together to stay at Addiscombe, the Surrey residence, the visit was a failure from Jane's point of view. Accustomed to be the brilliant woman in any company, she found herself outshone.

Lady Ashburton's personality was so shining that she was always the first attraction to those around, and she was considered to scatter pearls and diamonds whenever she spoke. Her essentially gay spirit, full of lightness and laughter and wit took the edge off Jane's sardonic humour in the shape of narrative embroidery, which was actually for once considered to be rather lengthy in comparison with the wit of Lady Ashburton, who never visibly attempted to hold the stage. Jane got only four hours sleep (she said) all the time she was there, and came away in a very sour frame of mind.

It rankled with her so much that soon after this the Carlyles had a very unpleasant row. Having said some violent and desperate things to him in her most biting manner, she left the house and went to Liverpool. She did not write to him. This threw him into a state of great anxiety and misery, and he begged for at least a line, if only to say that she had arrived safely. Meanwhile she had written to her close friend Mazzini, unburdening her troubles. He had replied, counselling restraint and forbearance, which helped her. At last she wrote softly to her husband, and he replied with pathetic humility and gratitude. Her birthday happened to fall just at this time but she got no letter from him : it had been mislaid at the post office. Now she was thrown into a pitiable state. It seems to have come as a frightful shock to her, not hearing from him that day. She walked back from the post office in a 'tumult of wretchedness' filled with all sorts of fancies – that he had not written on purpose, that she had lost him through excess of possessiveness, that he had gone to Addiscombe and found no leisure to remember her existence, that he was so ill that he could not write. She thought of rushing back to London to find out. Disdaining to conceal her feelings behind any show of indifference, she now took blame on herself (for the moment anyhow) saying, 'I know always, when I seem to you most exacting, that whatever happens to me is nothing like as bad as I deserve'. Then suddenly the letter came by special messenger. Her relief! 'Oh, my dear! I am not fit for living in the world with this organization. I am as broken to pieces by that little accident as if

I had come through an attack of cholera or typhus fever. I cannot even steady my hand to write decently.' And she ended by saying that she would try to believe that 'with all my faults and follies I am "dearer to you than any earthly creature" ', as he had said in his birthday letter, which could not have been more tender.

Nevertheless, he did not propose to cut himself off from the Ashburtons. He had received far too many kindnesses from both of them – Lord Ashburton had now long been an affectionate friend in whose company he delighted – to take so drastic a step without any explanation that would seem reasonable. Jane saw the sense in this, and she endeavoured for the next nine years – it was now 1846 – to restrain herself from any emphatic expression of disapproval. But it continued to rankle.

✗

25   *Domestic Help and Domestic Economy*

JANE CARLYLE once dropped the remark to her friend, Mrs
Russell, that 'strong-minded, able-bodied women are my aversion, and I run out of the road of one as I would from a mad
cow'. Her life would have been so much easier if she had been
more able-bodied and less dependent upon the good will of
servants. One day, when she was helping Anne Cook – one
of the main characters of the *dramatis personae* in the theatre of
the Carlylean staff – to wring some sheets, Anne flatly told her
that it was *'clean aboon yer fit'*. Jane ventured to claim that she
would get it by practice, and that weaker people than herself
had wrung sheets. *'May be sae,'* returned Anne coolly, *'but I
kenna where yeel find ony weaker, for a weaklier like cretur I
never saw in a' my life.'*

Only about a hundred years have passed, and yet we feel
almost as far away from the nineteenth century as from ancient
China in matters relating to transport, theology, sex, and servants. In those days the definition of a real lady was one who
had not been in her own kitchen for seven years. The servant or
servants did everything; the upper-class man or woman in the
drawing-room neither opened a window nor put more coal on
the fire, but rang for a maid to do so. There were considerate
masters and mistresses, but for the most part the servants were
wrongly regarded and underpaid; there was not enough *noblesse
oblige*, so time has taken its revenge in modern days when a
dreadful and truculent woman may come in *to oblige*. But there
were also mistresses who longed to have devoted retainers who
would stay for ever as almost one of the family. Jane Carlyle was
such a mistress, and nothing bears witness so undeniably to her
warm humanity as the love which some of her servants felt for
her. Helen Mitchell, who was with her for many years, would

hug and kiss her when she returned after an absence. But now, this very Helen suddenly decided to 'better herself'. She gave notice and left. Actually, she worsened herself by this, begged to come back and did so, but took to drink, was obliged to leave the Carlyles again, and soon died miserably. Broadly speaking, after Helen Mitchell there was an ever-recurring servant crisis, and a great many varied and strange characters came and went – who cannot be celebrated here.* It was often less like having assistants than difficult lodgers. Carlyle did realize how much they strained Jane's strength. 'My poor little sick partner,' he exclaimed, 'all this is *dirtier* for the mind than even the brushing of boots oneself would be for the body.' Fancy having to brush one's own boots! But he foresaw the time coming when there would be 'a determination on the part of wise people to do without servants'. That would be grand, he thought, 'had one been trained to do a little ordinary work'. *Trained?* Once he quoted Cobbett as saying, 'Dirt shall not be around me so long as I can handle a broom'. But Carlyle did not or could not handle one. Cobbett – what a contrast! This contemporary of his, another peasant's son, did such a prodigious amount of work of all sorts, and was such an influential genius that G. M. Trevelyan in his *Social History of England* puts one whole period under the head of 'The Age of William Cobbett'. He thought nothing of looking after a baby at the same time as writing a book! It is hard to conceive such a thing as a baby at Number 5 Cheyne Row. It is said that Jane Carlyle bitterly regretted having no children, and I'm sure she did, but the imagination weakens at the thought of what would then have followed in that house. Nero was about as much as could be managed.

Nero was a dog given to Jane by a friend in 1849, and he lived for ten years more with them. This dog considerably improved her health because of the great happiness he gave her; and when Nero died, her gratitude to those who took the trouble to understand her grief was boundless. Some people have thought that her attachment to this dog was excessive. But can we ever say that our love for animals is excessive? – especially

* See Thea Holme, *The Carlyles at Home*

for these strange beings whose saint-like patience with us, whose unvirtuous devotion and gladness of welcome bind up so many broken hearts. Certainly Nero must take his place in this history, if only to be mentioned in passing. Jane was fearful as to his reception by Carlyle. Once she had taken in a lost child, and was frightened lest he should know about it and start 'creating'. However, he took to Nero. 'To be sure,' said Jane in the vein she now adopted when referring to her husband, 'when he comes down gloomy in the mornings, or comes in wearied from his walk, the infatuated little beast dances round him on its hind legs as *I* ought to do and can't, and he feels flattered and surprised by such unwonted capers to his honour and glory.' But Carlyle's amiability was only spasmodic. If left alone to look after Nero when Jane was away, he became 'that vermin', or 'a real absurdity in this house', or the devil of a nuisance (very understandable) when he got lost during a walk. Then Carlyle would repent and report to Jane that 'Nero is sitting on the flagstones in the sunshine inquiring about lunch', a simple sentence yet strangely vivid and charming. Carlyle had a sympathy for animals. He tended to regard them as people. He had a good deal to do with horses: the reason why his health was so good, though he said it was so bad, was because of his continuous riding for hours a day even in London (just as Dickens would walk for what we would regard as enormous distances). He was a poor horseman, and might well have been thrown, as Sir Robert Peel was outside Buckingham Palace, and killed, but he had a certain rapport with his horses. He particularly liked Fritz because 'he had not been brought up to consider that the first duty of a horse was to say something witty'. He was convinced that Fritz held him in high esteem and had his best interests at heart, and that moreover he displayed an appreciation of sculpture.

If the servant problem was chronic, the more important problem of finance had consistently become less difficult. Carlyle made a calculation in his Journal in 1848 that he had some £1,500 in the bank, with an average of £300 coming in from his books, plus the £200 to £300 which yearly came in from what had been Mrs Welsh's estate, Jane having handed this over to him without the faintest desire to keep control of it herself. He said he was now rich enough. How rich, he asked, is Hudson, King of Railways? 'For certain quantities of yellow metal you can still command him to go lower than any shoeblack goes, to make himself an *unhangable swindler*.' But he was sorry for Hudson when a year later he fell into ruin and obloquy. 'It is now doubtful whether poor Hudson will have any money left. Perhaps that would be a real benefit to him. His brother-in-law has drowned himself at York. What a world this ever is! full of Nemesis, ruled by the Supernal, rebelled in by the Infernal, with prophetic tragedies as of old!' He himself could not be drawn by offers of big money. One day, when the Jew Bill was before Parliament, Baron Rothschild asked him to write a pamphlet in its favour, and offered to pay any sum he chose to ask. Carlyle courteously declined. In matters of principle and integrity he was as firm as steel. We should remember this when we think of his weaknesses. Thousands and thousands of strong-nerved men and satisfactory husbands and respectable pillars are as weak as water if offered easy money – *their* weakness then is wonderful to behold, and still more wonderful the smooth smiling plausible reasons by which they evade the slightest twinge of conscience and pocket the cash.

The fact that the Carlylean exchequer was now in a healthy state did not mean, however, that in practice they behaved accordingly. Far from it. If they visited Addiscombe, they walked from the station to save the cab fare. A sofa could not be bought without cautious haggling. When Jane travelled north, she took a cheap-class ticket and was very uncomfortable. Carlyle kept her short of house-keeping money : not intentionally, for he regarded her as 'the best of housewives; noble, too, in reference to the property which is *hers*, which she has never once in the most distant way seemed to know to be hers' – a remarkable fact calling for appreciation in deed rather than word. He gave her too little out of sheer vagueness, and she was unable to secure his attention when she advised him to alter the amount. In the end she found a remedy for this. She would use her pen. She had written down poultry; she had written down dogs; she had written down pianos – now she would write down an inadequate budget. So, sitting in a room below his, she composed a Statement of Household Accounts in her best literary style and most astringent vein of mockery in ironic protest, and then put it on his table for him to find when he returned from a ride. She entitled it *Budget of a Femme Incomprise.* It was 3,000 words in length, equal to a twenty-page pamphlet, and is doubtless unique in the history of exchanges between husband and wife on the not entirely happy topic of domestic economy. On coming in, Carlyle instantly read what he would not bother to *listen* to, enjoyed it immensely, not least the shrewing of himself, and at the foot of it wrote, 'Excellent, my dear clever Goody, thriftiest, wittiest, and cleverest of women. I will set thee up again to a certainty, and thy £30 more shall be granted, thy bits of debts paid, and thy will be done. T.C.'

26   *A Pleasant Task*

IN 1850 Carlyle took time off to write a book on his dear friend John Sterling, who had died in 1844. He was one of those men whose conversation, style, personality, character, idealism, and intellectual vigour make them dominating figures in their circle, sought-after, loved and welcomed. That is their art, their genius, we might say. The rest of the world does not hear of them; in old age they are have-beens, and after death, forgotten. For they have not channelled their talents into any public form in State, Church, Law, or Literature. They have had their ambitions in such directions, but have been too uncertain in aim to get anywhere, and, when they settle for literature, they find that they cannot write as effectively as they speak.

John Sterling, son of Edward Sterling, Editor of *The Times*, was a man of this sort, an exciting talker who longed also for action. His first essay in the field of action, with the idea of helping a Spanish insurrection, brought him a fearful shock, for not only was the action futile, but a relation whom he had persuaded to take part was captured and shot. In the mood that followed this disaster he was led to believe by a clergyman called Hare that his mission lay in the Church. For some time he had come under the influence of Coleridge who at this period was holding his famous monologues on Highgate Hill, strange discourses which while starting from no premise and arriving at no conclusion, yet seemed ever about to announce an ultimate in revelation. The weaker brethren were thus dazzled into that dread form of insincere sincerity by virtue of which we believe that we believe what we do not believe. Under this influence John Sterling became fair game for Hare, and once fallen among theologians, he allowed himself to be persuaded to get ordained. But after eight months as a clergyman, he gave it up and left the Church. He died young – for his constitution had always been fatally weak – and Hare wrote a biography of him. Carlyle was so grieved by this book, which focused upon Sterling merely as a clergyman, though that part of his life had in fact lasted but eight months, that he felt it as a duty to redress the balance. For Carlyle the fact that Sterling had only for such a brief period been able to embrace theological dogmas was one main cause of respect.

Carlyle never came out into the open regarding theology. He never said what he really thought in any sustained piece of writing. One gets the impression – perhaps rightly? – that he could not bear to pain his dear old mother, whose piety was such that she thought that God kept his eye on human conduct so closely that bad weather in Scotland was due to the exceptional sinfulness of the people. It would certainly have horrified old Mrs Carlyle had she come upon a little piece her son had written in his account of a short tour in Belgium in 1842. Entering a chapel in a cathedral at Ghent, he found 'a little closet of a place, perhaps some ten feet square and fifteen high. In the wall right opposite the entrance was a little niche, dizened round with curtains, laces, votive tablet of teeth, etc.; at the side of it, within the niche, sate a dizened paltry doll, some three feet long, done with paint, ribbons, and ruffles. This was the Mother of God. On the left lay a much smaller doll (literally, they were dolls such as children have). This was itself God. Good heavens! Oh, ancient earth and sky! Before this pair of dolls sate, in very deed, some half dozen women, not of the lowest class, some of them with young children, busy counting their beads, applying themselves to prayer. I gazed speechless – not in anger . . .' Carlyle never could take kindly to priests. After visiting another great church, he wrote, 'The Mass was over, but the worshippers, it seemed, still loitered. You could not say from their air that they were without devotion – yet they were painful to me. The fat priests, in whose real *sincerity*, not in whose *sincere cant*, I had more difficulty in believing, were worse than painful. I had a kind of hatred of them, a desire to kick them into the canals unless they ceased their fooling.'

In early days Carlyle had experienced his vision of glory, and he was able to get on for the rest of his life without benefit of clergy. He saw nothing to be gained by theological revivals or Oxford Movements, and was as ready to speak of 'the little ape called Keble' as to declare that Newman had 'the intellect of a moderate sized rabbit', rather in the same vein as he referred to 'the twaddling Lyell' on the scientific side, professing to see nothing in the evolutionist's claim that man was 'a fortunate orang-outang who had succeeded in rising in the world'. Disgusted by a scientific article in the *Fortnightly*, he commented – ' "A little lower than the angels," said Psalmist David; "a little higher than the tadpoles," says Evangelist ———. These people bring you what appears the whitest beautifullest flour to bake your bread with, but when you examine it you find it is *powdered glass,* and deadly poison.'

That last remark sums up fairly well the feeling of depression which the 'mechanistic' philosophy of the time caused in religious men – the feeling that Darwinism was 'banishing mind from the universe'. Yet really Carlyle knew better, or had known better, than this. He knew that neither theologians nor scientists could destroy the religious vision. He knew that the insight that came with the faculty of *wonder* was all we really need. He knew that 'Awe is the highest thing in man,' as Goethe put it, 'and if the pure phenomenon awakens awe in him he should be content; he can be aware of nothing higher and he should seek nothing beyond : here is the limit'. He knew that there is no answer to the riddle of the world, save to be able to see the world : 'Fear no *seeing* man,' he wrote to John Sterling; 'know that *he* is in heaven, whoever else be not; that the arch-enemy, as I say, is the arch-stupid. I call this my fortieth Church Article, which absorbs into it and covers up in silence all the other thirty-nine.' He knew that we must not seek salvation, but that vision *is* salvation. He knew that given this faculty there is no problem concerning the 'miraculous' on the one hand and the 'material' on the other; that the miracle of water is greater than any turning of water into wine. He knew that the natural is more supernatural than the 'supernatural', just as the ordinary is more extraordinary than the 'extraordinary'. Remember how* when he was unknown and unpraised, feeling his power while raging at his chains, he had exhorted himself – 'Wait thou on the bounties of thy unseen Taskmaster, on the hests of thy inward Daemon, and neither fear thou that this thy great message of the Natural *being* the Supernatural will wholly perish unuttered'. He felt *all* nature to be alive and divine, the 'inorganic' as much as the organic – *not* seeing 'life' as a little cyst in the midst of dead matter. When he had written, 'That the Supernatural differs not from the Natural is a great Truth (grasped by modern philosophers), but they went far wrong however, in this, that instead of raising the natural to the supernatural, they strove to sink the supernatural to the natural,' he was saying something strikingly close to what was said much more elaborately by the scientist and dynamic thinker, James Hinton, in his book *Life in Nature* published in 1862.† He insisted, with excitement, that 'there is *nothing more* in the organic than in the inorganic. All the inorganic – *all Nature* – is living.' If we fancy that matter is 'dead', Hinton argued, our vision is faulty, and the deadness is in us. He said that it was absurd to suppose that a 'materialistic' explanation to life should deprive it of its glory or take away its 'spiritual' exaltation. 'You are faced,' he said to the depressed victim of 'materialistic' science, 'by a small ingot you believe to be gold and a large mass you believe to be clay, and you are told that they are both of the same nature. You jump to the conclusion that they are both clay. *But what I can prove to you is that they are both gold!*' That is the core of Hinton's *Life in Nature*. It is also the core of what Carlyle wished to say. But he did not say it. Instead he wrote six volumes on Frederick the Great!

You may think that he did not say it because he could not

---

* See page 64

† Latest edition published in 1932 by Allen & Unwin with a remarkable introduction by Havelock Ellis

say it – being lacking in scientific equipment. He could have said a good deal, and been very helpful. We must not forget his massive knowledge, his matchless industry, and his flair for mathematics before ever he took up literature. 'He had mastered the *Principia*,' says John Tyndall, 'and was well aware of the vast revolutionary change wrought, not in Science only, but in the whole world of thought, by the theory of gravitation'. Tyndall wished that Carlyle had written upon Newton or Boyle: 'Had he taken either of them in hand, he would undoubtedly have turned out an impressive figure'. Tyndall held that it was a mistake to suppose that Carlyle's mind was unscientific. He said that he had had many calm and reasonable conversations with him about Darwinism and kindred subjects, 'and I could see that his real protest was against being hemmed in. . . . "Yes, Friends," he says in *Sartor*, "not our Logical Mensurative faculty, but our Imaginative one is King over us".' Further, Tyndall had this to say: 'The scientific reader of his works must have noticed the surprising accuracy of the metaphors he derived from Science. Without sound knowledge such uniform exactitude would not have been possible. He laid the whole body of the sciences under contribution – Astronomy, from the nebular theory onwards; mathematics, physics, chemistry, geology, natural history – drawing illustrations from all of them, grinding the appropriate parts of each of them into paint for his marvellous pictures. Quite as clearly as the professed physicist he grasped the principle of Continuity, and saw the interdependence of "parts" in the "Stupendous Whole". To him the Universe was not a Mechanism, but an Organism – each part of it thrilling and responding sympathetically with all other parts. Igdrasil, the Tree of Existence, was his favourite image: "Considering how human things circulate each inextricably in communication with all, I find no similitude so true as this of a tree. Beautiful; altogether beautiful, and great. The *Machine* of the Universe, – alas, do but think of that in contrast!" ' John Tyndall's word is not one to take lightly. One feels that Carlyle, instead of writing on Frederick, could have given us something akin to Macneile Dixon's marvellous book, *The Human Situation*.

However, in his *Life of Sterling* he was not particularly concerned with preaching anything, but only in rescuing his friend from narrow judgements after his death – which indeed he did more effectively than his endeavour to rescue Edward Irving from delusions during his life. In his Introduction he said, 'All men are to an unspeakable degree brothers, each man's life a strange emblem of every man's; and that Human Portraits, faithfully drawn, are of all pictures the welcomest on human walls. Monitions and moralities enough may lie in this small Work, if honestly written and honestly read; – and, in particular, if my image of John Sterling and his Pilgrimage through our poor Nineteenth Century be one day wanted by the world, and they can find some shadow of a true image here, my swift scribbling (which shall be very swift and immediate) may prove useful by and by.'

'My swift scribbling' : there are curiously paradoxical aspects to Carlyle, the writer and the man. As we know, he made very heavy weather over the composition of most of his books, shamefully so, we cannot fail to feel, for he behaved in this, as in so many matters, as a spoilt child who had never been told to shut up and think of others. But once he let drop the remark that only when writing did he really feel alive. Exactly; that is a common feeling amongst born writers. In fact he loved writing as much as he loved talking, and should never have permitted himself to complain out loud, to squeal, at the pains also involved. He enjoyed writing so much that he wrote what amounts to many extra volumes – in the form of letters and journals – in which some of his best things appear. In his *Life of John Sterling* there occurs what is probably the best known passage he ever wrote, beginning, 'Coleridge sat on the brow of Highgate Hill . . .' The pen of the artist is slanted at an angle as idiosyncratic, and as effective, as that of Dickens. One feels that the passage came easily and naturally to him – for nearly all the best passages of any author are achieved without strain. That set piece on Coleridge on Highgate Hill is too well known to need quoting here, but we may note an entry he made in his Journal regarding Coleridge's *Table Talk*, which he considered 'a great possibility that has not realized itself'. One is reminded irresistibly of H. G. Wells's 'dead kitten' remark concerning Henry James*. 'Never did I see such apparatus,' says Carlyle, 'got ready for thinking, and so little thought. He mounts scaffolding, pulleys, tackle, gathers all the tools in the neighbourhood with labour, with noise, demonstrations, precept, abuse, and sets – three bricks.' John Carlyle said that the effort of writing was always very great for his brother because 'he wrote with his heart's blood in a state of fevered tension,' and Carlyle himself declared that 'a paroxysm of clairvoyance' was indispensable to get the work done properly. Well, we need not question all of this; the impact which he finally made upon his period was due to the *élan* on his page – and it makes the re-writing of the French Revolution manuscript all the more heroic and extraordinary. All the same, we are bound to note that when the artist had free play without strain and was in no paroxysm, he often did extremely well. Emerson once wrote to Carlyle, 'Nothing seems hid from those wonderful eyes of yours; those devouring eyes; those thirsty eyes; those portrait-eating, portrait-painting eyes of thine'. And it is certainly true that it was as a portrait-artist that he excelled. I think he was at his best in lightning sketches, which he obviously threw off without effort. He made many such sketches while on his travels: a washerwoman seen from the wayside, a poor worn-out old couple returning home by ship – when his tenderness was as noticeable as his lack of sentimentality. His imagery is really memorable. Here is a hungry man: 'A man not far from me, a weak-built figure, almost *without chin*, shovelled and forked with astonishing alacrity out of the stew-pan, his protrusive eyes flashing all the while, and his loose eyebrows shuttling and jerking at every stroke, the whole face of him a devouring Chimaera. He gave

---

* '...The thing his novel is *about* is always there. It is like a church lit but without a congregation to distract you, with every light and line focussed on the high alter. And on the alter, very reverently placed, intensely there, is a dead kitten, an egg-shell, a bit of string...'
In Boon by H. G. Wells, Society of Art and Literature, pp. 106-7

the remnant – a small one, I doubt – to his boy, snatched up the black bread, and made a cut in it at the first bite equal to a moderate horse-shoe.' Was ever sheer appetite made so visible by words?

Every generation contains its Sterlings. During his lifetime Carlyle sometimes spoke of John's 'argumentative babblation'; but he recognized the great qualities of his friend, and was determined to rescue him from the shades, to make him visible to many others – and this he nobly stepped aside to do. 'Here, visible to myself, for some while, was a brilliant human presence, distinguishable, honourable and lovable amid the din of common populations; among the million little beautiful, once more a beautiful human soul : whom I, among others, recognized and lovingly walked with, while the years and the hours were.'

27   *Carlyle as Traveller and Visitor*

A PATTERN began to emerge in the two Carlyles' art of not living together too much. There were the regular vast house upheavals, when Carlyle was sent away. These upheavals were rather distressing for him at times, especially when workmen fell through his bedroom ceiling. 'This repairing of my house has been a dreadful thing, tumbling topsy-turvy all my old habits etc,' he complained. In so far as he could not set to work on the most ambitious task he was to undertake, a history of Frederick the Great, without perfect quiet, it was necessary to construct a soundproof room – an operation involving a good deal of topsy-turvyism! He was very grateful to Jane for her efforts and accomplishments in house improvement – in one letter he expressed that gratitude in such decided terms as should have satisfied her for ever. But there was something excessive about it all. 'Seas of paint still flooding everything, and my poor Jane so beaten in her hard battle . . .', he begins one entry in his Journal. Was it always necessary? It seems strange.

Jane, as we have seen, vastly preferred to ride the tumult alone, and was eager to get him out of the house until it was all over. He went to Scotland, to Ireland, to Wales, to the Lake District. For him a simple journey was always a terrible venture. He did not disembark at a pier – he was 'flung into the street'. He did not go to rest in a sleeping berth – that was impossible. *'This way to gents cabin'*, he saw written up on a ship. He had a look. Gents' cabin! Good God, some gents, some cabin! – 'gent packed on gent, few inches between the nose of one gent and the nape of the other gent's neck'. Not for him. He sought the deck – only to find 'chaos come again'. And on arriving at his destination his hosts did not always find him easy to please. In the Lake District, at the house of his friends, the Marshalls, where the Tennysons were also staying, he explained that on account of being kept awake by 'poultry, children, and flunkeys', he must leave next day. His room was changed, and in the morning, after a good sleep, he looked from his window to see the sun shining over lakes and mountains – imagine it! Naturally he now wanted to remain. But he had overdone it. His hosts did not properly grasp that he had changed his mind; and, amazingly, he didn't know how to climb down with a hearty laugh at himself, he probably just dithered – and had to go. A sad incident – for they did not want him to go. He was so well loved that all who really knew him delighted to minister to his comfort. His temperamental fits were more than balanced out by his conversation, 'his talk was so intensely interesting, so intensely entertaining, says Froude. He could be so amusing that even the servants at places where he dined sometimes ran from the room choking down their laughter. That side of this most curious man is lost to us now, not easily discernible from his books or his letters. We know his humour, but not his laughter.

Jane Carlyle had no inner funds of this kind. With her it was wit or gloom. That gloom was real, not at all rhetorical, as his often was. That made it possible for her to compose one of the best short pieces ever written upon the pathos of the past. She revisited Haddington in 1849, and left an account of her visit. Carlyle came upon it after her death, and refers to it as 'very interesting'. It is far more than that. It is a masterpiece. It wrings the heart. It is personal and it is universal. It mirrors the anguish of all those who, returning upon the scenes of their youth, walk back through the injured years and face the disfigured hopes that have been set aside*.

Throughout these years, Carlyle intermittently visited the Ashburtons in their residences at Addiscombe or The Grange or Bath House. This was a pleasure that he was unwilling to forgo. Also, and this was very human in him, he could never really forget how he had studied German and read Faust in a ditch at Annandale; and by his own exertions was now courted and coddled in the houses of the great, receiving the applause of the

* See Carlyle, *Letters*, Vol. III, p. 146 ff.

applauded and the love of lovely Ladies. He could not deny himself limelight at Bath House to meet there on equal terms all sorts of Eminences, grey or otherwise, and it gave him particular pleasure meeting Sir Robert Peel whom he liked for the significant reason that the old statesman exhibited a vein of *drollery*; and the exchange of courtesies between them concerning his *Cromwell* was on both sides as striking in the warmth of the regard as in the felicity of the expressions.

He went to these grand house-parties because he could not resist the general idea and the particular lure of Lady Ashburton. But too much of it did not suit him at all. Of course it was part of the act to groan : he felt he owed it to himself to utter cries of woe on all occasions. But it certainly was something of an endurance test for anyone not accustomed to that sort of thing. The organized idleness, the doing-nothingism, extending for days, called for a training he had not acquired. He could never accustom himself to the 'great tumults of servants and equipments'. He would not have denied that cows and sheep have the right to demand their valets in terms of cow-men and sheep-men, but for us to claim the same privilege and to have men's men he undoubtedly considered ludicrous. Though an old-fashioned bed with curtains was 'a rare blessing', Carlyle could never reconcile himself to having his precarious sleep broken by the appearance of a footman bringing him newly-creased trousers. He would hanker after the very different scheme of things at Scotsbrig and report to his old mother, 'a long nightmare; *folly* and *indigestion* the order of the day'. Yet he answered the call of the Ashburtons even to the extent of joining them at their shooting-box in the Highlands, when the aim of his hosts was to rough it and enjoy a modicum of discomfort in primitive conditions so as to balance the excessive luxury of their existence elsewhere. Carlyle, requiring no such balance and never wishing to shoot birds for fun, was hopelessly out of place, and his groans were justified. And yet he went !

Nothing bears witness so plainly to the spell which the Ashburtons exercised over him than the fact that he failed to go at once to Scotsbrig when his mother was ill and likely to die.

She was now in her eighties, a very remarkable old lady who still rode a horse and bathed in the sea. She was immensely proud of her famous son who never failed to write long letters to her on all subjects, and insisted upon her accepting sums of money from time to time. She was nearly as proud of her daughter-in-law, delighting in her wonderful letters, reading them over and over until it seemed that she knew them by heart. But she may not have relished a postscript which Jane added to a letter from Carlyle to her in the summer of 1852, since it has a touch of asperity – and is well worth noting as we pass :

'It is quite true that he is done with that illness, and might have been done with it much sooner if he had treated himself with ordinary sense. I am surprised that so good and sensible a woman as yourself should have brought up her son so badly that he should not know what patience and self-denial mean – merely observing "Thou'st gey ill to deal wi' ". Gey ill indeed, and always the longer the worse. When he was ill this last time, he said to Anne one morning, "I should like tea for breakfast this morning, *but you need not hurry*". The fact was, he was purposing to wash all over with soap and water; but Anne didn't know that, and thought he must be dangerously ill, that he should ever have thought of saying *you needn't hurry*. "It was such an unlikely thing for the master to say, that it quite made my flesh creep." You see the kind of thing we still go on with.'

Old Mrs Carlyle had become bewildered when years went by and Jane did not join her husband on any visit to her. She sensed trouble, and would repeat wryly, 'I would ha' liked weel to see Janie ance mair,' and 'I would like right weel to have a crack with Janie ance mair'. She was made sad when Jane, after the death of Mrs Welsh, began to address her as 'Dear Mrs Carlyle' instead of 'Dear Mother'. It is a great pity that Jane could not have seen more of her mother-in-law. When she was alone at Cheyne Row she sometimes – dutifully – accepted an invitation to go to the Ashburtons at Addiscombe. But Lady

Ashburton did not like her; thought her hypochondriacal; considered that wine was bad for her; prevented her from going to bed when she had a headache; and, though she suffered from cold, did not allow the rule to be broken that no fires should be lit early in the autumn – a maid removing the coals when she lit one herself in her room! When Carlyle told his mother about this, she was as angry as amazed, 'that the puir creature could n' get a bit fire! not so much as a bit of fire for a' their grandeur'.

However, Jane did go to Scotsbrig by herself late in 1852; but it was not a very successful visit, for the family fell out with one another, and with her, regarding the best assistance for Mrs Carlyle who had fallen very ill. In the following year it seemed almost certain that she was dying. Carlyle was at the Ashburtons at the time, and *delayed* in setting out for Scotland! Luckily he arrived just in time to be able to speak to his mother before she died. Had he been too late, his remissness would have inflicted a wound upon him which would never have healed.

✡

28 The Monstrous Task

HE now set himself to spend thirteen to fourteen years writing
the six volumes on Frederick the Great. Possibly no book
ever caused an author so much trouble, or so many expressions of misery, or so much pain to those around him. Yet it
was not worth writing this *magnum opus* at all. It is a sad
experience to visit the house in Cheyne Row – now open to
the public – and go upstairs to the soundproof room much
as he left it over eighty years ago. There is a musty
melancholy in the silent uninhabited room, and the volumes
of *Frederick* in a book-case give an impression of great
bleakness.

The book is not read now. When it came out it was, of
course, widely reviewed and highly praised, and considered as
a Monument. Certainly, as a massive Pillar, it completed and
supported an impressive reputation. We are still told by
'authorities' that 'there are many magnificent accounts of
battles: Rossbach might be replaced by Mollwitz or
Dettingen or Leuthen or a dozen others'. I do not care who
won those battles, for I have been defeated by them – on
paper. They are not magnificent. Still, they are 'essential
reading', we are told, 'for all students of military history' –
what a fate. Yet it goes without saying that there are
many passages of portraiture or pathos when the great
artist makes his characteristic effects. The Electress Louisa
bids farewell to the Elector: 'At the moment of her death, it
is said, when speech had fled, he felt from her hand, which
lay in his, three slight slight pressures – farewell thrice
mutely spoken in that manner, not easily to forget in this
world.' Such lines of simplicity and power came from the
intensely emotional nature of the author, whose tenderness

was blocked, hopelessly damned by Scottish dourness, only breaking the bounds when it was too late. 'Oh, my Feekin! oh, my Feekin! whom have I in the world but thee?' cried his Friedrich Wilhelm in self-revulsion – shades of the shape of things at Cheyne Row, shades of the last lonely road when there would be no 'Feekin'!

It is impressive, always so, to note how Carlyle employs in his character painting his hard-won minutiae of fact. When Friedrich Wilhelm becomes King he sacks most of the sycophants and lackeys and flunkeys and superfluous official persons. He settles for 'three active Pages, sometimes two, instead of perhaps three-dozen idle that there used to be. In King Friedrich's time, there were wont to be a Thousand saddle-horses at corn and hay: but how many of them were in actual use? Very many of them were mere imaginary quadrupeds; their price and keep pocketed by some knavish *Stallmeister*, Equerry, or Head-groom. Friedrich Wilhelm keeps only Thirty Horses . . .' And how clearly is the character of the new king shown immediately after the death of his father. He hurried to a private room and sat there alone, in tears, thinking of his life with his father, their estrangement, their reconciliation, the great virtues of the dead man. 'All in tears he sits at present, meditating these sad things. In a little while the Old Dessauer, about to leave for Dessau, ventures to the Crown Prince, Crown Prince no longer; "embraces his knees", offers weeping his condolence, his congratulation; hopes withal that his sons and he will be continued in their old posts, and that he the Old Dessauer, "will have the same authority as in the late reign". Friedrich's eyes, at this last clause, flash out tearless, strangely Olympian. "In your posts I have no thought of making change; in your posts yes; and as to authority I know of none there can be but what resides in the king that is sovereign", which, as it were, struck the breath out of the Old Dessauer; and sent him home with a painful miscellany of feelings, astonishment not wanting among them.'

So we could continue multiplying examples; yet the work

cannot be read as a whole – which is the only way an important book can legitimately be read. It is far too wearisome. There is no question of being carried on under the impetus of the style, whereas, if we read Gibbon, we long for time to complete all the volumes; or with Macaulay, whether we like his tone or not, we are swept forward. If a volume were published consisting of pieces (from a few lines to a page) selected from *Frederick* for their pictorial or emotional power, we would doubtless be surprised at the riches. We would also be horrified at the thought of so much energy, so much skill spent upon the creation of things shut away like jewellery in never-opened safes.

Why did he write it? When he wrote *The French Revolution* he believed that he could show that there were 'Forces in the universe to destroy what was rotten'. He continued to believe this, claiming that the universe is so constructed that it is Right only that is strong – and *Frederick the Great* was supposed to emphasize this further. Unfortunately this was not clear to everyone, and his critics accused him of believing in nothing but the divine right of strength. When the historian, Lecky, taunted him with this he loftily commented – 'With respect to that poor heresy of might being the symbol of right "to a certain great and venerable author," I shall have to tell Lecky one day that quite the converse or *reverse* is the great and venerable author's real opinion – namely that right is the eternal symbol of might;' and he went on to claim that no son of Adam was more contemptuous than himself of might 'except where it rests upon the above origin'. But, since we can never be sure when might is resting upon right or just resting upon might itself, we are largely dealing with empty words. Carlyle took up *Frederick* because he was a German scholar and could here deploy his knowledge, and because he sensed that Germany had an important future to play in Europe – though he had no faint inkling of what a 1914 or a 1938 would bring forth from that quarter! It is clear that the whole chore got out of hand; he began to feel dislike of his chosen hero, to yearn to get finished with him, and to be dismayed to find that another volume and then another was necessary. He really knew that he had gone astray. But he could not face the fact. He could not now call a halt. He could not swerve from his rightful course. At last the book was finished – amidst the shambles of his domestic life. It was acclaimed and then neglected, and regarded by its author for all the last years of his life with bewilderment, remorse, and misery. How different from his feelings at the conclusion of *The French Revolution* !

29 Tragedy

MEANWHILE, though, as we have seen, it was never a good idea for the Carlyles to attempt to go anywhere together, in 1852 they thought they would try a water-cure at Malvern under the guidance of a Dr Gully. This was scarcely a cure for Carlyleism. Very soon he discovered that for him 'water taken as a medicine was the most destructive drug he had ever tried'. He might as well have swallowed knives or bathed in boiling oil. Writing a letter from the spa at this time, Macaulay said, 'Carlyle is here undergoing a water-cure. I have not seen him yet, but his water-doctor said the other day, "You wonder at his eccentric opinions and style. It is all stomach. I shall set him to rights. He will go away quite a different person." If he goes away writing common sense and good English, I shall declare myself a convert to Hydropathy.' Macaulay was a startlingly talented and powerful writer; and, on occasion, no man wielded a stick with more effect – especially when he had got hold of the wrong end of it. But he was not the right man to act as interpreter of Carlyle's stomach. Carlyle had a number of things to say about him, not all of them complimentary. Here is one note : 'Essentially irremediable, commonplace nature of the man; all that was in him now gone to the tongue; a squat, thickset, low-browed, short, grizzled little man of fifty. These be thy gods, oh Israel !'

The Carlyles tried another change of scene together in 1855, accepting from the Ashburtons the free use of their Addiscombe house while they were absent. But shortly after their arrival, Jane disappeared. She had risen before breakfast in a fit of spleen, and without a word of explanation had returned to Cheyne Row. Carlyle wrote to her in a humble, pathetic vein, which no doubt she expected and desired – tenderly and sadly missing her.

By this time, one of the Addiscombe servants had become an Hyena, and another a Dragon. He expressed the hope that she would come back for a day or so if only to grapple with the cook.

The truth is that Jane Carlyle had been becoming increasingly depressed and angry concerning Carlyle and Lady Ashburton. It was understood that she would accompany her husband on his visits to Addiscombe and elsewhere, but more often she refused to go. She took little pleasure in wealthy establishments, declaring that 'the superior splendour is over-balanced by the inferior comfort'. She disliked dressing up and sitting down to table with women with bare shoulders. She protested that rather than attend at a 'magnificent ball' she would prefer to be with hay-makers in the country. Her attitude antagonized Lady Ashburton, who made little attempt to mollify her, and on one occasion, when they were all travelling north together, drew a class distinction by reserving a special railway carriage for herself – a slight which was never forgiven. Jane, very justly and sanely, claimed the right to have as many men friends as she chose; such as Sterling and Mazzini, whom she loved, and Godefroi Cavaignac, whom she romantically wor-shipped. Carlyle was not seriously attracted by any other woman till Lady Ashburton appeared, an attachment which had no danger of passion in it. Yet Jane's jealousy was not without reason : for if *she* asked him to plan, do, or go anywhere, she was met with 'if's and possibly's and 'probably's and 'perhaps'es and hummings and hawings; whereas at the summons of Lady Ashburton he showed no indecision, but at once complied with her behests. In 1845, after the publication of *Cromwell*, he had written, 'Good be with thee, dear little Goody mine. "We clamb the hill together" in a thorny but not paltry way. Now let us sit and look around a little.' That was on paper : in practice, he sat with Lady Ashburton. He was now proposing to climb another hill, *Frederick the Great* (which climb took thirteen years and ensured Jane's early death), and would no doubt seek refresh-ment from the same quarter. She had to put up with the malicious tittle-tattle of Rogers, a fashionable diner-out of the day. She had to swallow the fact that Carlyle *now* gave German lessons to Lady Ashburton. It was too painful to contemplate time's twisting: in the days of their courting she had condescended to him, and, while ridiculing his accent to his face and before his friends, had said, 'apply your talents to overcome the inequality of our births'; and now, in the houses of the aristocracy, *she* was regarded as a piece of his luggage and rather a nuisance. In the old days he had praised her genius as a writer, now he never encouraged her, never realized the brilliance of her letters, and even declared that she knew nothing about grammar! If she felt the resentment of frustration, she had cause. She could not know that the time would come when her *Letters* would be more widely read than his *Frederick*.

As time went on now, she began to make cutting remarks about him in her circle of friends. She had always done this, even in his presence, and he would laugh heartily; but the vein of mockery was getting sour, and her remarks on marriage, which in earlier days had been light, were less so now, as when she wrote to Forster that she thought there was much truth in the idea that 'marriage is a shockingly immoral institution, as well as what we have long known it for – an extremely disagreeable one;' and having asked him to send her a current novelist's book she expressed intense interest in it, declaring that it was a long time since she had come upon a novel of this sort, 'all about love, and nothing else whatever. It quite reminds me of one's own love's young dream. I like it, and I like the poor girl who can still believe, or even believe that she believes all that. God help her!'

Up to this period her letters to him had been signed as 'Yours affectionately', or 'ever affectionately', and sometimes 'Janekin', or 'Jane C.', or 'Goody' or 'Your Adorable Wife'. Now she began to end distantly worded letters to him with 'Yours faithfully', contrasting with her passionately affectionate ones to her dear friend Mrs Russell of Holm Hill, Scotland, in one of which she gave an appallingly vivid and sinister picture of Carlyle and herself at the breakfast table, '. . . Mr C. at one end of the table, looking remarkably bilious; Mrs C. at the other, looking half dead . . .' Her letters to him grew very sad, how she had lonely thoughts by night and day, how he no longer wanted her, how he was better off without her 'so far as company goes' and how she suffered from the consciousness of that – 'God knows how gladly I would be sweet-tempered and cheerful-hearted, and all that sort of thing for your single sake, if my temper were not soured and my heart saddened beyond my own power to mend them'. Carlyle, sunk hopelessly under the weight of the terrible book he had elected to write, did not comprehend this. 'Oh', he sighed, 'if you could but cease being conscious of what your company is to me! The consciousness is *all* the malady in that.' He said mildly that her letters were 'sombre and distrustful perhaps beyond need'. He felt, indeed truly, that she did not know him. 'Oh Jeannie you know nothing about me just now', he insisted. 'With all the clearness of your vision, your lynx eyes do not reach into the inner regions of me, and know not what is in my heart, what, on the whole, was always, and will always be there, I wish you did, I wish you did.' But, strangely, he couldn't say his feelings in person, he couldn't *show* them in practice. They were all bottled up, just as his father's for his wife had been.

Knowing that she had nothing to fear from his friendship with Lady Ashburton, he thought Jane's indignation unreasonable, saw no point in giving in to it, and did not even take precautions against ambivalence of statement. In the late summer of 1856 he had been having a very restful time with his family in Scotland, but had begun to feel guilty and out of place there when the harvest was on. He didn't like twiddling his thumbs in the midst of so much activity. It never occurred to this peasant's son that he might have lent a hand at the harvest and felt a lot the better for it – in interesting contrast, again, with Tolstoy, the aristocrat's son, who found it essential for him to do 'an honest day's work' of this kind as often as he could. So he said he would now return to Cheyne Row, unless he accepted an invitation from the Ashburtons to join them at Loch Luichart, which 'he would avoid if he could. That is the whole truth'. As it was not the whole truth, since he did not wish to avoid it, he went to the

Loch. From there he sought to cheer Jane up by sending her an account of his discomforts : how he was enfeebled by lack of potatoes; how Lady Ashburton was 'in a worse humour than usual'; how, for the sake of economy, she wouldn't let him have a fire in his room and got angry if he sought to set up 'a peat from its flat posture'; how he had nothing to do or say or read or think, his only resource being ten-mile walks in the rain, a return to the house tired out, and being obliged to fill in the time before dinner by going to bed in a dressing-gown, a scarf, a mackintosh and a hat.

Jane was not amused – nor impressed. She replied harshly and truly, saying that she took it he was pretty comfortable; that if he went to a place it was because he chose to go, and stayed because he chose to stay, since it was not his habit to sacrifice himself for the pleasure of others. She said it was unnecessary for him to pretend a wish to be at home, for she didn't believe him, and ended with words which throw a sudden searing light upon scenes between them normally evaded from mention in correspondence : 'If I were inclined to believe you, I should only have to call to mind the beautiful letters you wrote to me during your former visit to the Ashburtons in the Highlands, and which you afterwards disavowed and trampled into the fire !'

They both had their eye on posterity, carefully preserving letters, journals, and notes; but they never lifted the lid too high. At the worst Ashburton period Jane had made up her mind to go away, and even to marry another person. Once she told him what a close thing this had been. His comment hurt her more than anything he had ever said to her : 'Well, I do not know that I should have missed you; I was very busy just then with Cromwell'. In his essay on Carlyle, Lytton Strachey wrote – 'It is impossible not to wish that she had indeed fled as she intended with the unknown man of her choice. The blow to Carlyle's egoism would have been so dramatic, and the upheaval in that well-conducted world so satisfactory to contemplate !'

She now began to keep a Journal – (1855-1856). She was aware that it was a risky thing to do. It inclined to 'egoistical babblement' and could lead to 'whatever is factitious and morbid in you'. She hoped to avoid this, and certainly she made her approach in a very different spirit from that in which the Countess Tolstoy wrote her Diary. She recalled a remark made by Charles Buller concerning the murder of the Duchess de Praslin – 'What could a poor fellow do with a wife who kept a journal but murder her?' Yet she was resolved to indulge herself, she said, on the principle of the Scottish professor who drank whisky simply because he liked it. Her Journal is not all about her feelings and wrongs; there are some of her best objective things to be found in it – but the main purpose was *cri de coeurism*, as she well knew.

The general tone of it is set soon enough with the entry, 'That eternal Bath House. I wonder how many thousand miles Mr C has walked between there and here, putting it all together; setting up always another milestone betwixt himself and me. Oh, good gracious! when I first noticed that heavy yellow house without knowing, or caring to know, who it belonged to, how far I was from dreaming that through years and years I should carry every stone's weight of it on my heart.' The next entry begins, 'A stormy day within doors, so I walked out early, and walked, walked, walked'. This is closely followed by a similar view : 'Fine weather outside, but inside blowing the devil of a gale'. Next day, all she entered was, 'Alone this evening. Lady A. in town again; and Mr C. of course at Bath House'. She adds a quotation :

> 'When I think of what I is
> And what I used to was
> I gin to think I've sold myself
> For very little cas.'

Two days later she is reminded of her mother's death – 'Oh, my mother! nobody sees when I am suffering now; I have learnt to suffer "all to myself" '. That was true. It was hard for an only child to travel that way. She quotes the saddest of all Scottish ballads :

> 'Oh, little did my mother think
> The day she cradled me,
> The lands I was to travel in,
> The death I was to dee.'

Such was the timbre of this private Journal. On 29 May 1856, she made her so far most emphatic comment on marriage: 'Mr B.', she wrote (whoever he may have been), 'says that nine-tenths of the misery of human life proceeds according to his observation from the institution of marriage. He should say from the demoralization, the desecration of the institution of marriage, and then I should cordially agree with him.'

There was another entry which was withheld by Froude in the edition of her *Letters and Memorials*, though it had not been omitted by Carlyle in his editing. It is a passage which referred to certain blue marks on her arms. In the course of a violent quarrel concerning the Ashburton affair, she so provoked him by her stinging words about his enslavement to a 'great Lady', as she saw it, that he struck her – which left blue marks on her arms.

So miserable did she feel during these years, so hopeless, that once she resolved to put herself out of the way altogether. She often went by sea when she visited Scotland. Another sea-journey had been planned. She had determined, under cover of night, to drop over the stern and thus disappear in such a way that it could be interpreted as an accident. Something prevented the journey, but Geraldine Jewsbury was entirely convinced that, had she gone that way, she would never have been seen again*.

There is no knowing how far the estrangement would have gone had not Lady Ashburton unexpectedly died in 1857. She remains rather a misty figure for us. She was no letter writer, so we cannot find her that way. Nor can we capture her from witty remarks which she is supposed to have made, for they have not come down, and thus she has not talked herself into life for us. Imperial rich women are inclined to differ from the ordinary species, or they are a species of their own, and behave in a

* See Appendix, p. 180.

manner all their own. Carlyle said, many times, that she was 'the most queen-like woman' he had ever known or seen. To the end of his life he insisted that 'the honour of her constant regard had for ten years been among my proudest and most valued possessions'. It is hard to fathom exactly what he felt about her emotionally. At the time of the 'magnificent ball' which she gave and to which, very much out of character, he wanted to go and insisted upon Jane going with him, he wrote to her as 'a glorious Queen. It is something to have seen such a one, and been seen by her, though only as if from precipice to precipice, with horrid chasms, and roaring cataracts, and black rivers of Acheron flowing between for ever.' At another time, she was 'the only one glow of radiancy that still looks of heaven to me, on a ground which is black and waste as the realm of Phlegethon and Styx'. In short, very enjoyable in terms of tragic dramatics.

�֍

30 Calamity

SHORTLY after the death of Lady Ashburton, Jane made another
Scottish visit. The shadow never completely passed away, but
her letters now became affectionate again. In one of them she
told him that she now fell into a fearful state of nerves when his
letters arrived; she said she turned sick at the sight, that she
would catch at a chair and tremble before opening one, in case
there might be some word in the letter that 'I would rather
hadn't been there'. This is more strange than if Carlyle had been
afraid of opening *her* letters!

Back in Chelsea, two months later, she became ill again, and
did her best to conceal it as usual, though at the same time she
observed to a friend that 'until a woman cries men never think
she can be suffering'. Nevertheless, it is clear that Carlyle put
great restraint on himself not to make her worse. For at this
time there was another severe outbreak of servant trouble, and
he insisted that had it not been for 'the devil's brood of house
servants', she would be well again, and he exclaimed to John,
'Poor little soul! I have seldom seen anybody weaker, hardly
ever anybody keeping *on foot* on weaker terms'. Meanwhile, he
kept grinding on with *Frederick*, and the first two volumes were
nearly done. 'What a magnificent book this is going to be!', she
had written to him as she read it in manuscript, 'the best of all
your books.' He was as much touched by the generosity of her
spirit as he was encouraged by her judgement. Coming in from
his ride or walk, when they were together at Cheyne Row, he
would often talk *Frederick*. On three successive evenings he
talked about the Battle of Molwitz. A few years later she told
him how, as she listened to him, her thought was – 'Alas, I shall
never see this come to print: I am hastening towards death
instead!'

Having finished those two volumes, Carlyle was again in a state of collapse, and went to Scotland once more to his family for a rest, prior to setting forth to Germany yet again to visit another lot of battlefields. Meanwhile from Scotland he wrote to his wife more tenderly than he had ever done before : 'Take care, take care of thy poor little self, for truly enough I have no other.' As the days passed, and he was wrapped in the stillness of his northern fortress, he again reflected upon his married life and how hard it had been for her. He wrote letter after letter of love and of sorrow and of remorse for his misdeeds. Rehearsing in his mind his habitual want of restraint, accusing memories came before him. 'It is as if the scales were falling from my eyes, and I were beginning to see, in this my solitude, things that touch me to the very quick. . . Past, present, future, yielded no light point anywhere . . . My poor, heavy-laden, brave, uncomplaining Jeannie! Oh, forgive me, forgive me for the much I have thoughtlessly done and omitted, far, far, at all times, from the poor purpose of my mind . . . what a suffering thou hast had, and how nobly borne! with a simplicity, a silence, courage, and patient heroism which are only now too evident to me . . . if it please God there are yet good years ahead of us . . .'

Jane did not respond to these letters with much warmth. She shared with deeply affectionate natures a tendency to be unforgiving, in contrast with the easy forget-and-forgive complacency of shallow people, which is often as worthless as the tolerance of those who are merely indifferent. Once, when telling Carlyle how kind his brother, Jamie, and sister-in-law, Isabella, had been to her, she said with true knowledge of herself, 'I never forget kindness, nor, alas! unkindness either!' And now, as often happens between married couples who do not get on very well, the woman's heart had grown harder towards her husband, and his softer towards her. Not that Jane's letters were unaffectionate in reply, but she had ceased to take his declarations very seriously. She had accused him in the past, and no doubt still clung to the idea, that he wrote letters with an eye to future biographers. He had rejected the idea with indignation, but of course there was something in it, though not in relation to these letters in 1858, and I think that Jane occasionally cast her eye in the same direction, for surely no woman would have written that brochure of 3,000 words on Domestic Economy, and a particularly careful and brilliant account of a visit to a Taxation Official, unless she hoped for a public larger than the figure one.

Anyway, Jane was justified in the doubt she felt about 'better days ahead', or indeed of any meaning in the words except as a sort of theme-song or prayer. For when he returned from Germany he was back to normal. It was extraordinary. When he was at a distance, he got everything into perspective. Once he wrote to Jane, 'Last night, at dinner, Richard Milnes made them all laugh with a saying of yours. "When the wife has influenza, it is *a slight cold* – when the man has it, it is etc, etc." ' He could laugh at himself, he could not mend himself. He was like a child, incapable of restraint, and full of remorse afterwards for his outbursts. And now again her nerves were shattered by his behaviour. 'If Mr C. wakes once in a night', she wrote to a friend (and never, by the way, did she refer to him as far as I can see, either to himself or to his mother or to anyone else, as Tom, or Thomas – he had, strictly, no Christian name), 'If Mr C. wakes once in a night he will complain for a week. I wake thirty times a night but that is nothing.' If his liver was out of order it was worse than anything that had befallen a member of the human race.

Once more they made the mistake of attempting a joint holiday at a place called Humbie in Scotland. Jane declared that it was there like living in a madhouse. Her state of mind at this time is mirrored in the reply she gave to a letter she got from a young friend called Miss Barnes. On opening it she had all but screamed, she said. It had positively taken away her breath. 'You had looked to me such a happy, happy little girl!' The shattering news in the letter had been that Miss Barnes was going to be married. Jane dared not congratulate her, it would be tempting Providence. 'The triumphal-procession-air which, in our manners and customs, is given to marriage at the outset – that singing of *Te Deum* before the battle has begun – has, ever since I could reflect, struck me as somewhat senseless and somewhat impious. If ever one is to pray – if ever one is to feel grave and anxious – if ever one is to shrink from vain show and vain babble – surely it is just on the occasion of two human beings binding themselves to one another, for better or for worse, till death part them.'

In the following year, 1860, having again reduced her and himself to a tatter of nerves, Carlyle went off to another friend in Scotland at Thurso Castle, and presently suggested that Jane go for a change of air to his sister at the Gill. No sooner had she set out than he misled her into thinking that he intended to return to Cheyne Row just at that time : and consequently she herself returned, on the ground that he couldn't possibly shift for himself there without her for twelve hours, and 'fancy your coming home to a curtainless bed'. Both of them were furious. She, because of the carelessness of statement that had created the misunderstanding; he, because of her 'precipitancy' and 'rashness' and 'infatuated conduct', and the assumption that he was some kind of goat or polar bear needing a keeper. Yet she was justified. For in the next year, when she had fled from Frederick to the care of her most cherished friend, Geraldine Jewsbury, at Ramsgate, 'the letter that came from him every morning was like the letter of a Babe in the Wood, who would be found buried with dead leaves by robins if I didn't look to it.' Scarcely an exaggeration, for he had said that he felt 'like a child *wishing mammy back*' – his words, his italics. 'It was the face of a lost child, says Havelock Ellis in *The Dance of Life*. Do we see something of this in Whistler's famous portrait? And when he got back he behaved wildly again, or even more so. Frederick was driving him mad.

Frederick was not alive : indeed, only a book, *Frederick The Great* – but alive enough to destroy the living. It has been given various names – the Nightmare, the Dragon, the Minotaur, the Unutterable Book. It made a frontal attack upon his stomach. In a panic Jane prepared special sorts of soups, puddings, cutlets, and cakes without butter in them, for a man she was afraid to meet at breakfast and glad to avoid at dinner. In a panic she tried to stand between him and the servants when he raged about food being turned to poison by 'that horse!', 'that moon-calf!', 'that cow!', 'that brute who will be the death of me!' In vain did she steel herself to face the effects of his lumbago, which gave him perfect liberty, she declared, to be as ugly and stupid and disagreeable as ever he liked. As the months passed, her own health began to break down more completely than ever before. Her right arm became almost paralyzed. She sensed the approach of death. Old-time friends calling at the house did not recognize her when she came to the door. Strangers in railway carriages offered her assistance. Doctors told her that she must keep away from Carlyle. When she was away, friends beseeched her to stay away. A woman signing herself 'Mi' wrote to her, 'I hope you do not think of returning home. Should Mr Carlyle become rampageous I will set Mrs Fergusson on to pray for him.' But Jane did not wish to give in, she had taken on this task, it had been her life work; *Frederick the Great* was not going to stop her, she would *endure to the end*. Yet at moments she faltered : 'I sometimes feel as if I should like to run away'. But the old question arose which always arises with married couples tempted to separate on their last lap, and in so many cases is the deciding factor against flight : and so she added, 'But the question always rises, Where to?'

Then suddenly – it was as sudden as surprising – Carlyle realized what a strain he had been putting upon her, and became much more considerate at last. When, during the summer of 1862, she was staying with her dear friend, Mrs Russell, at Holm Hill, he ceased complaining about anything. He implored her not to pinch herself over money. He assured her that all was well with him at Cheyne Row, his work, his sleep, his food, the staff, everything. When she returned he kept it up, getting on with the third and fourth volumes of *Frederick* without groaning. He insisted that she should have two servants instead of one. He ordered a carriage to be at her disposal two or three times a week. Between the first and second part of the day's work, he rode or walked for some hours. 'On his return,' to quote a few words from Froude which have always attracted attention, 'he would lie down in his dressing-gown by the